SOUTH YORKSHIRE SUPERTRAM

FARES AND TICKETING
1994-1997

A COMPILATION OF
TABLES AND DIAGRAMS

DAVE ASPINWALL

The Transport Ticket Society
2000

Front cover:

Supertram 01 at Meadowhall on 21 March 1994 - the first day of operation. Ticket from last batch of vending machines to be closed down. These were at Meadowhall Interchange during the early evening of 1 July 1997.

[Dave Aspinwall]

Rear cover:

Supertram approaching Fitzalan Square / Ponds Forge on 19 March 1994, two days before the start of public operations. Row of Abberfield Technology ticket machines visible under the tramstop shelter. Ticket was validated in one machine which was specially programmed to print a 12-digit serial number during August and September 1995.

[Dave Aspinwall]

*Comments etc. regarding this publication are welcome;
please write to the Society's Publications Officer:*

David Harman
24 Frankfield Rise
Tunbridge Wells
TN2 5LF

E-Mail: David.Harman@btinternet.com

© Copyright Dave Aspinwall, 2000

ISBN 0 903209 34 9

Published by
The Transport Ticket Society
81 Pilgrims Way, Kemsing, Sevenoaks, TN15 6TD

Printed by
Paterson Printing Ltd,
Tunbridge Wells

Contents

1	Introduction	2
2	Ticketing Chronology	3
3	Staged Opening Dates	7
4	Tramstop Codes to late February / early March 1996	8
5	Tramstop Codes from late February / early March 1996 to 25 October 1997	9
6	Fare Structures	10
7	Ticket Types	21
8	Validation Styles from Blue Vending Machines	37
9	Tramstop Codes - Validations from Blue Vending Machines	40
10	Validations from Yellow Validating Machines	44
11	Validation Styles - Wayfarer 3 Machines	49
12	Keyboard Layouts - Wayfarer 3 Machines	51

In the short space of something less than four years a remarkable variety of tickets has appeared in use on this new Light Rail Transit system with its complement of only 25 tramcar units. Neglecting the finer points of detail, about 140 different collectable ticket types and associated items can be identified.

The original ticketing system was designed around the use of a unique type of Australian ticket machine manufactured by Abberfield Technology. At each tramstop two types of machine were installed: blue vending (ticket dispensing) machines and yellow machines solely for the purpose of validating tickets. Initially these latter machines were used for providing a second validation of tickets purchased from the vending machines and also for the validation of tickets pre-purchased from various agents' outlets. At the commencement of operations in March 1994 the vending machines printed full validating details of the date and time of issue so that the requirement for a second validation from the yellow machines was superfluous and time consuming. As a result, and also to speed up ticket issue, the time, date and tramstop code were de-programmed from the vending machines in July 1994. However, it still remained necessary to separately validate tickets bought from the vending machines in the validating machines. This laborious system was finally simplified and rationalised at the end of July 1995 with the reprogramming of the vending machines to produce full validating data on the tickets and the abandonment of the requirement for separate validation in the yellow machines.

However, there remained other problems associated with the originally devised ticketing system. Apart from the driver, the trams were unmanned and revenue collection depended upon passengers' honesty with ticket inspection being a somewhat intermittent and random activity. There is no doubt that the system was abused significantly and much revenue lost as a result thereof. Also, the vending machines were the target of persistent vandalism. The situation was so serious that the machines on a long section of the Halfway branch were closed down after only six month's use. As an interim measure conductor operation with Almex machines was introduced on this section. Following this, Wayfarer Clipper machines were trialled in early 1996.

In order to overcome the above described problems it was decided to convert the whole system to conductor operation using Wayfarer Clipper machines. Conversion started in June 1996 followed by a series of vending machine closures between June and October 1996. Some little-used validating machines were also closed in late 1996. After this some vending machines at a limited number of tramstops and the majority of the original validating machines remained in use until the end of June 1997 when all machines of both types were finally closed down.

Apart from ticket sales from the tramstop vending machines, the original ticketing policy was designed around the complementary sale of tickets from various agents' outlets such as South Yorkshire Transport Executive's offices and newsagents. It had been intended that each outlet would validate tickets in a special type of Wayfarer Mark 3 machine. These machines were supplied prior to commencement of operations in March 1994 but were not put into general use until August 1994 when they were installed at SYPTE Travel Shops and a limited number of retail outlets. This method of ticket issue proved to be time-consuming and much of the validating data was superfluous either because the tickets required a second validation at the tramstop or because the ticket price was, in any case, pre-printed on the card tickets. This system was abandoned in August 1995.

As the tramway system developed, with many changes in the fare structure, the agency tickets went through a remarkable series of changes. The most popular tickets were those that offered a discount over tickets purchased from the tramstop vending machines. With the introduction of conductor operation in June 1996 the sale of agency tickets declined rapidly with only the discount tickets remaining popular. At the original time of writing, January 1998, agency-sold tickets remained available from a limited number of outlets.

At the commencement of operations in March 1994, tickets bore reference to South Yorkshire Supertram (No.2) Limited; (No. 2) referred to the operating company and (No.1) to the construction company. This latter company was subsequently renamed South Yorkshire Light Rail and the (No.2) company title simplified to South Yorkshire Supertram Limited. On 20 December 1997 Stagecoach took over the operation of the trams and network.

The tables and diagrams presented in this publication are intended to be complementary to the reports which have appeared in the *Journal* of The Transport Ticket Society over the period of May 1994 to January 1998. In aggregate these reports amount to about thirty-five pages of A4 script. The reader is referred to these reports, along with a selection of illustrations included in this publication.

The author will be grateful to receive examples, either actual or photocopied, of any tickets which fall outside the ranges listed in the tables.

Dave Aspinwall
Sheffield
April 2000
dadwasp@btinternet.com

1994	
Mon 21 Mar 1994	Stage 1 opening, Fitzalan Square to Meadowhall Interchange. First range of tickets, by Booth, introduced.
Mon 23 May 1994	Royal opening. Commemorative ticket.
Mid Jul 1994	Reprogramming of vending machines to show fare and date only. First noted 15 Jul 1994
Mon 22 Aug 1994	Stage 2 opening, Fitzalan Square to Spring Lane and Arena/Stadium. New range of tickets, by Orion, introduced
Autumn 1994	Special Event validated tickets introduced.
Mon 5 Dec 1994	Stage 3 opening, Spring Lane to Gleadless Townend. Introduction of £1.15, £1.20, £1.30 colour coded tickets.
1995	
Tue 3 Jan 1995	Opening of Parkway Central Park and Ride facility.
Mid-Jan 1995	Reprogramming of some vending machines to show fare only. First noted 12 Jan 1995
Sat 18 Feb 1995	Stage 4A opening, Fitzalan Square to Cathedral.
Mon 27 Feb 1995	Stage 4B opening, Cathedral to Shalesmoor.
Sun 26 Mar 1995	Stage 5A opening, Gleadless Townend to Halfway. Free travel (Mother's Day!)
Mon 27 Mar 1995	Stage 5A - fare paying commenced.
Mon 3 Apr 1995	Stage 5B opening, Gleadless Townend to Herdings Park.
Mon 1 May 1995	'Special Offers', with adjustments of fare structure, introduced.

Abberfield Technology blue ticket vending machine (left) and yellow validating machine (right) at Shalesmoor tramstop on 23 October 1995, the opening day of the final stage.

[Dave Aspinwall]

Mon 19 Jun 1995	Joint arrangement with Mainline Buses introduced - Rotherham to Meadowhall to Sheffield City Centre and return. Subsequently abandoned.
Sat 1 Jul 1995	Park and Ride - £2.00 daily increased to £2.50. £10 Weekly introduced.
Late Jul 1995	Reprogramming of vending machines to show full validating data including tramstop code.
Tue 1 Aug 1995	Official introduction of full ticket validation by blue vending machines and cessation of requirement for separate validation of tramstop purchased tickets in yellow validating machines. Special Offer of reduction of £1.50 fare to £1.00 introduced.
Mon 14 Aug 1995	Park and Ride - Introduction of Multi-pack tickets.
Mon 21 Aug 1995	Tramstop ticket promotion introduced - McDonald's - expiry 15.10.95.
Late Aug 1995	Withdrawal of Wayfarer 3 machines.
Mon 4 Sep 1995	Fare restructuring. Introduction of 90p and £1.00 (6 for price of 5, 13 for price of 10). Introduction of CITY RETURN on Birley Moor Road to Halfway section (available from tramstop vending machines only)
Sat 7 Oct 1995	Park and Ride - Daily price reduced to £1.25 for 6 consecutive Saturdays.
Sun 8 Oct 1995	Park and Ride - Kiosk burgled and 3 new sets of tickets in revised colours introduced following the incident.
Thur 12 Oct 1995	Almex introduced on Halfway section following vandalism of ticket machines.
Mon 23 Oct 1995	Stage 6 opening, Shalesmoor to Middlewood/Malin Bridge. Free travel for 3 days.
Thur 26 Oct 1995	Stage 6 - fare paying commenced. CITY SAME DAY RETURN facilities extended and Agents' ECAR ticket introduced.
Nov 1995	Introduction of dedicated SPECIAL EVENT tickets (ASPEC, CSPEC)
Nov 1995	Closure of vending machines on Halfway section following persistent vandalism.
Sat 18 Nov 1995	Park and Ride - Free on Saturdays to 23 Dec 1995
Mon 11 Dec 1995	Introduction of Free Christmas Special ticket available to 2 Jan 1996

1996

Mon 29 Jan 1996	7 DAY NETWORKER introduced.
Mon 5 Feb 1996	Tramstop ticket promotion - UCI Cinemas (Crystal Peaks) (Adult only) - expiry 28.3.96.
Mid-Feb 1996	Trial use of Wayfarer Clipper.
27 Feb 1996 - 2 Mar 1996	Reprogramming of vending and validating machines to show 3 letter tramstop code.
Sun 3 Mar 1996	Concession fares raised from 15p/25p to 20p/30p.
Mon 18 Mar 1996	Tramstop ticket promotion - McDonald's - expiry 28.04.96
Early Apr 1996	Co-op promotion
Early May 1996	NETWORKER TRAVELCARDS (Weekly, Monthly, Quarterly) introduced.
Early Jun 1996	Wayfarer Clipper production machines introduced for conductor training.
Sun 9 Jun 1996	Opening of Park and Ride facility at MIDDLEWOOD.
by 10 Jun 1996	BR facility for combined rail and Supertram travel available.
Sun 16 Jun 1996	Almex withdrawn.
Mon 17 Jun 1996	Conductor operation with Clipper machines commenced Sheffield Station/Hallam University to Halfway. Clipper NETWORKER laminated card introduced. Fare restructuring - introduction of 80p CITY SINGLE.
Sun 30 Jun 1996	Closure of vending machines Granville Road to Spring Lane and Herdings/Leighton Road.
by Jul 1996	New Visitor ticket introduced.
Jul 1996	All validating machines finally reprogrammed into standard format.
Mid-Jul 1996	Promotions/concessions at Middlewood Park and Ride.
Aug 1996	Clipper roll with red text introduced for Special Events.
Early Sep 1996	Closure of vending machines on Meadowhall branch.
Mon 16 Sep 1996	Introduction of Exchange class on Clipper machines.
18/19 Sep 1996	Closure of further vending machines on Halfway branch.

Sep/Oct 1996	Swimming Baths promotion.
Sat 28 Sep 1996	Student Networker (£1.50) introduced - available only from Clipper machines.
by 30 Sep 1996	80p CITY SINGLE extended to Herdings/Leighton Road and Herdings Park.
Early Oct 1996	Promotion - ASDN Networker cards.
12/13 Oct 1996	Closure of vending machines on Middlewood Branch.
Mid-Oct-mid Nov	Selective closure of yellow validating machines.
Pre-Xmas 1996	Promotions/concessions at Park and Ride sites.
Mon 2 Dec 1996	Introduction of Free Christmas Special ticket available to 2 JAN 1997.
Early Dec 1996	New SIT BACK AND RELAX Clipper roll introduced.
Xmas period	Promotion - Marks and Spencer from Park and Ride sites. Art Galleries and Museums promotions.

1997

Jan 1997	Snow White and Seven Dwarfs promotion.
Late Jan 1997	Promotion - Coupons for free evening travel.
Mon 17 Feb 1997	Routing structure revised. New 7 DAY NETWORKER Clipper laminated card introduced.
Feb 1997	Further ASDN promotions (half price)
Feb 1997	Further Marks and Spencer Promotions (Park and Ride)
Mon 3 Mar 1997	New set of multi-coloured Park and Ride tickets introduced including Monthly tickets.
Tue 1 Apr 1997	Child fare raised from 20p to 30p. Revised ECSC ticket introduced.
Sat 10 May 1997	Closure of PARKWAY P+R site
Mon 12 May 1997	Opening of NUNNERY SQUARE P+R site. Introduction of Magnetic cards. Various offers.
Mon 2 Jun 1997	Re-opening of PARKWAY P+R site
end Jun 1997	Wayfarer Clipper first promotional rolls - TSB
Mon 30 Jun 1997 and Tue 1 Jul 1997	Final closure of tramstop vending and validating machines

30 June 1997
Both red lights are lit which means the machines are still
live, although the vending machine coin-slot is blanked- off.
[Dave Aspinwall]

Tue 1 Jul 1997	Introduction of Multi-pack booklets of tokens at NUNNERY SQUARE P+R site
Early Jul 1997	£1.50 Return for special events introduced
Mon 28 July 1997	Multi-pack booklets of tokens also made available at PARKWAY and MIDDLEWOOD sites
End Jul 1997	Special Event (ie red text) Clipper rolls universally in use
Mon 4 Aug 1997	Electronic barriers introduced at MIDDLEWOOD P+R site. Magnetic cards introduced
Mon 1 Sep 1997	First fares increase. New issue of ECAS (£1). New Cover Cards for ECAT multi-packs. £2 Return introduced
Thur 4 Sep 1997	Wayfarer Clipper promotional roll - SAFE
Mid Sep 1997	PARKWAY P+R renamed Cricket Inn.
Mon 15 Sep 1997	JOBSEEKER introduced.
Sun 26 Oct 1997	Clipper machines reprogrammed into new geographical style (Jobseeker class - may have been introduced earlier)
Mon 27 Oct 1997	Purple route extended into City Centre
Sat 8 Nov 1997	Reappearance of ASPEC Special Event ticket
Sat 15 Nov 1997	At all P+R sites:- £1 for car+driver on Saturdays to 27 Dec 1997
Mon 17 Nov 1997	£0.60 Child and Senior Citizen Returns introduced
Same week	Coupons giving evening travel for 50p - to 31 Dec 1997.
Mon 24 Nov 1997	HALFWAY P+R site opens. Discounts until 31 Dec 1997.
Mon 1 Dec 1997	Discount vouchers (from interim timetable) available to 31 Dec 1997:- 7 Day Networker and £2 Return
Sat 20 Dec 1997	Stagecoach takes over South Yorkshire Supertram Ltd

30 June 1997
Notice on yellow validation machine announcing the
introduction of on-tram ticket issue by conductors.
[Dave Aspinwall]

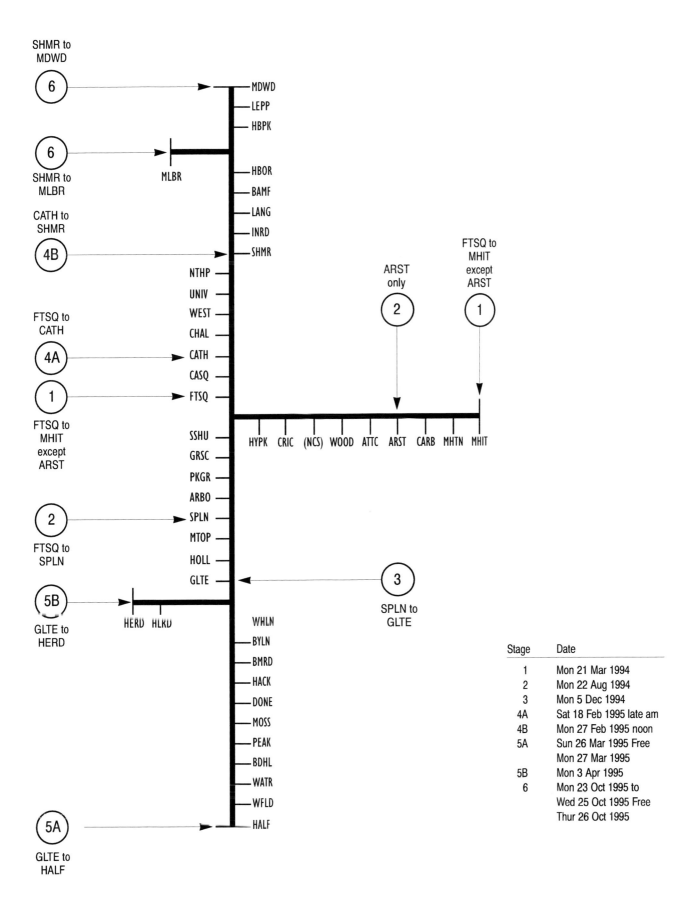

Stage	Date
1	Mon 21 Mar 1994
2	Mon 22 Aug 1994
3	Mon 5 Dec 1994
4A	Sat 18 Feb 1995 late am
4B	Mon 27 Feb 1995 noon
5A	Sun 26 Mar 1995 Free
	Mon 27 Mar 1995
5B	Mon 3 Apr 1995
6	Mon 23 Oct 1995 to
	Wed 25 Oct 1995 Free
	Thur 26 Oct 1995

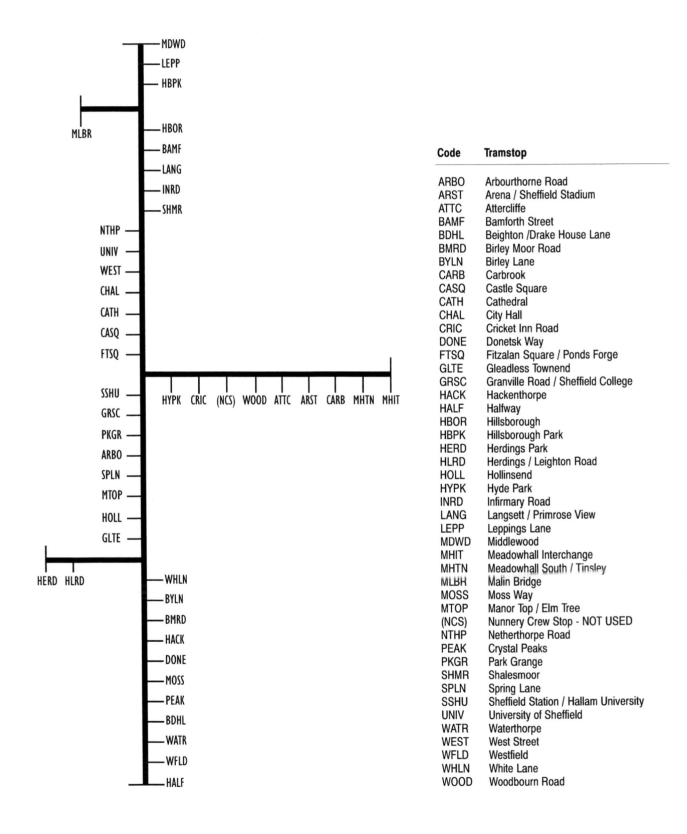

Code	Tramstop
ARBO	Arbourthorne Road
ARST	Arena / Sheffield Stadium
ATTC	Attercliffe
BAMF	Bamforth Street
BDHL	Beighton /Drake House Lane
BMRD	Birley Moor Road
BYLN	Birley Lane
CARB	Carbrook
CASQ	Castle Square
CATH	Cathedral
CHAL	City Hall
CRIC	Cricket Inn Road
DONE	Donetsk Way
FTSQ	Fitzalan Square / Ponds Forge
GLTE	Gleadless Townend
GRSC	Granville Road / Sheffield College
HACK	Hackenthorpe
HALF	Halfway
HBOR	Hillsborough
HBPK	Hillsborough Park
HERD	Herdings Park
HLRD	Herdings / Leighton Road
HOLL	Hollinsend
HYPK	Hyde Park
INRD	Infirmary Road
LANG	Langsett / Primrose View
LEPP	Leppings Lane
MDWD	Middlewood
MHIT	Meadowhall Interchange
MHTN	Meadowhall South / Tinsley
MLBR	Malin Bridge
MOSS	Moss Way
MTOP	Manor Top / Elm Tree
(NCS)	Nunnery Crew Stop - NOT USED
NTHP	Netherthorpe Road
PEAK	Crystal Peaks
PKGR	Park Grange
SHMR	Shalesmoor
SPLN	Spring Lane
SSHU	Sheffield Station / Hallam University
UNIV	University of Sheffield
WATR	Waterthorpe
WEST	West Street
WFLD	Westfield
WHLN	White Lane
WOOD	Woodbourn Road

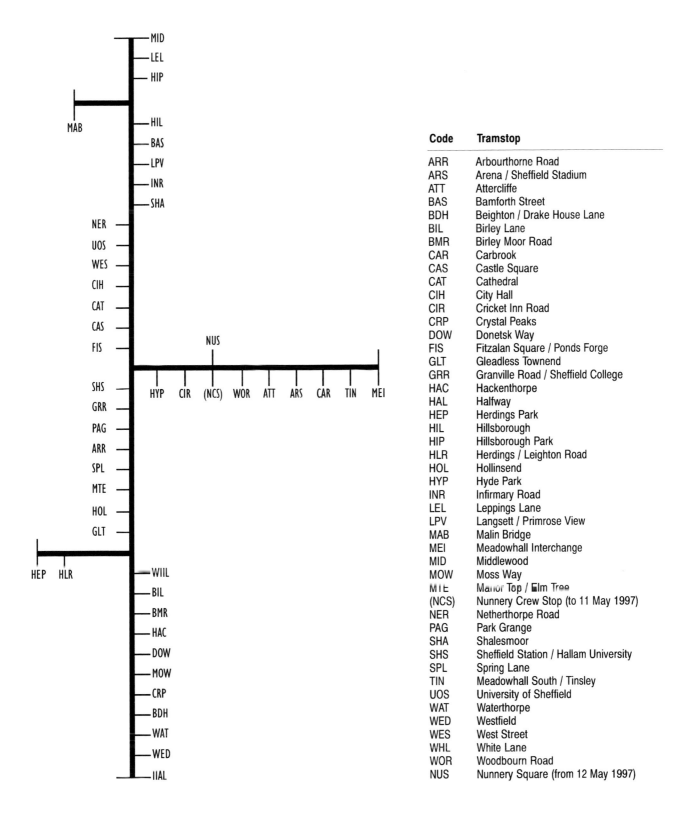

Code	Tramstop
ARR	Arbourthorne Road
ARS	Arena / Sheffield Stadium
ATT	Attercliffe
BAS	Bamforth Street
BDH	Beighton / Drake House Lane
BIL	Birley Lane
BMR	Birley Moor Road
CAR	Carbrook
CAS	Castle Square
CAT	Cathedral
CIH	City Hall
CIR	Cricket Inn Road
CRP	Crystal Peaks
DOW	Donetsk Way
FIS	Fitzalan Square / Ponds Forge
GLT	Gleadless Townend
GRR	Granville Road / Sheffield College
HAC	Hackenthorpe
HAL	Halfway
HEP	Herdings Park
HIL	Hillsborough
HIP	Hillsborough Park
HLR	Herdings / Leighton Road
HOL	Hollinsend
HYP	Hyde Park
INR	Infirmary Road
LEL	Leppings Lane
LPV	Langsett / Primrose View
MAB	Malin Bridge
MEI	Meadowhall Interchange
MID	Middlewood
MOW	Moss Way
MTE	Manor Top / Elm Tree
(NCS)	Nunnery Crew Stop (to 11 May 1997)
NER	Netherthorpe Road
PAG	Park Grange
SHA	Shalesmoor
SHS	Sheffield Station / Hallam University
SPL	Spring Lane
TIN	Meadowhall South / Tinsley
UOS	University of Sheffield
WAT	Waterthorpe
WED	Westfield
WES	West Street
WHL	White Lane
WOR	Woodbourn Road
NUS	Nunnery Square (from 12 May 1997)

PERIOD I

Adult Tramstop Prices

  21 Mar 1994   FTSQ to MHIT opening.

  21 Aug 1994   Period end.

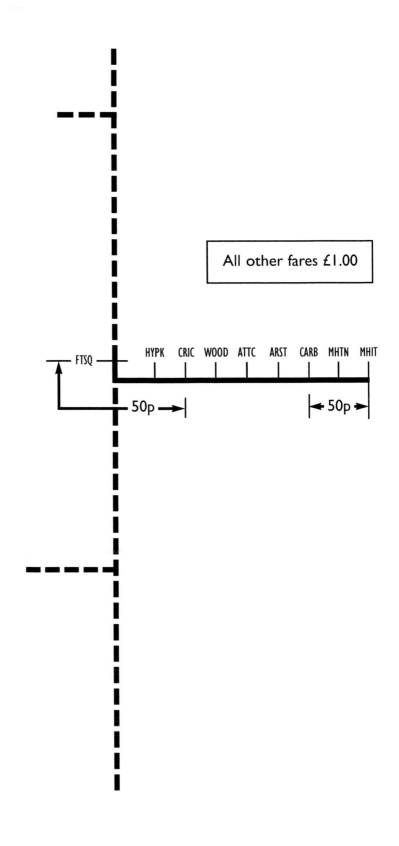

All other fares £1.00

PERIOD 2

Adult Tramstop Prices

  22 Aug 1994   FTSQ to SPLN opening + ARST.

   4 Dec 1994   Period end.

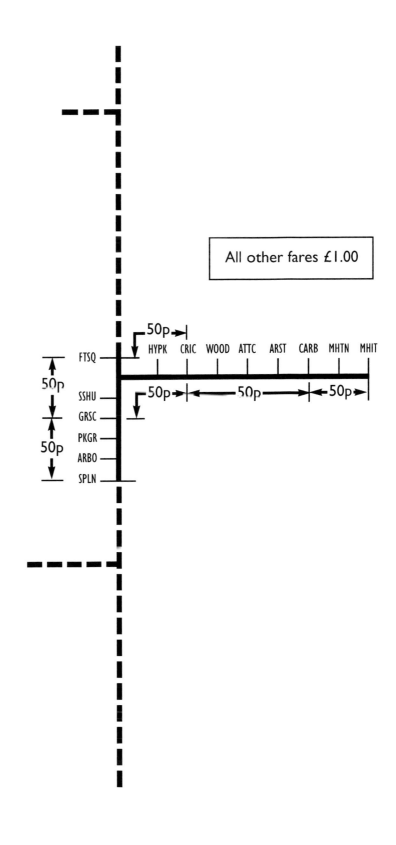

PERIOD 3

Adult Tramstop Prices

5 Dec 1994   SPLN to GLTE opening.

18 Feb 1995   Period end.

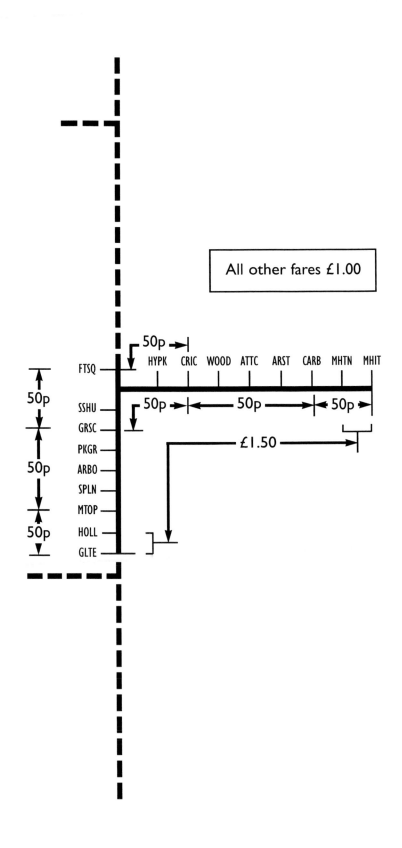

PERIOD 4

Adult Tramstop Prices

18 Feb 1995   FTSQ to CATH opening (am).

21 Feb 1995   CATH to SHMR opening (noon).

26 Mar 1995   Period end.

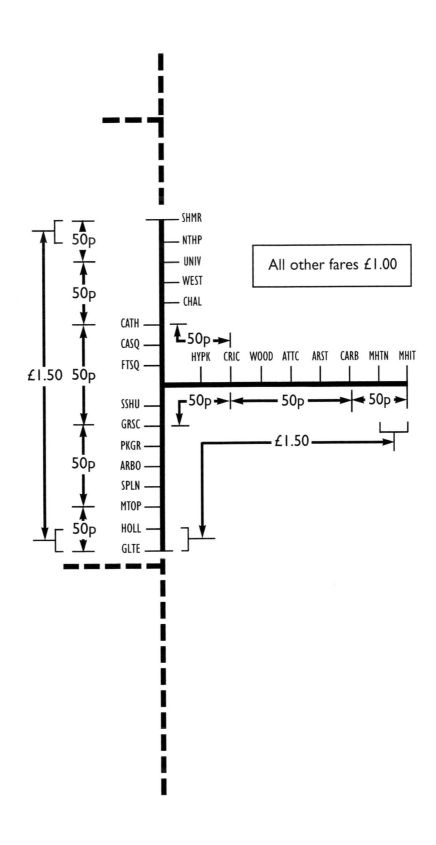

All other fares £1.00

PERIOD 5

Adult Tramstop Prices

27 Mar 1995   GLTE to HALF opening.

3 Apr 1995   GLTE to HERD opening.

30 Apr 1995   Period end.

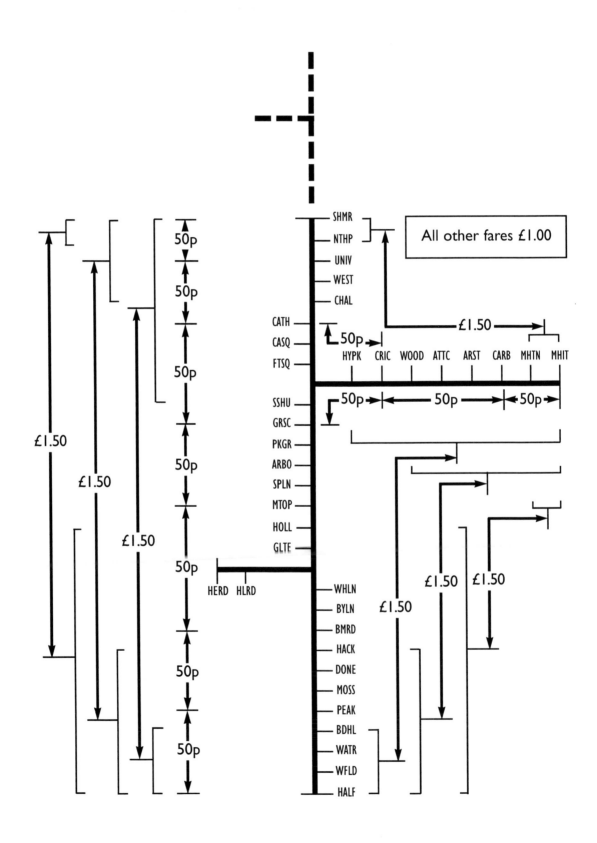

PERIOD 6

Adult Tramstop Prices

   1 May 1995   Period start.

  31 Jul 1995   Period end.

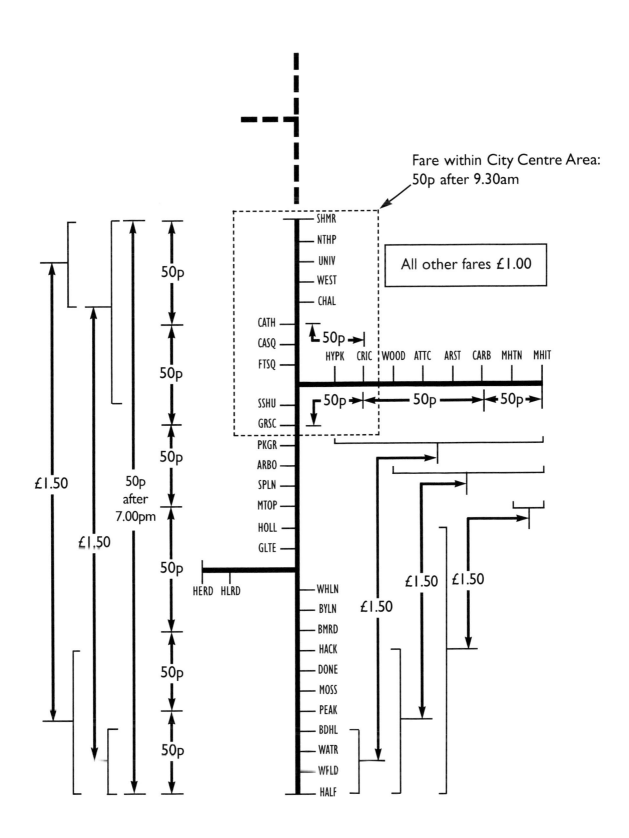

Fare within City Centre Area:
50p after 9.30am

All other fares £1.00

PERIOD 7

Adult Tramstop Prices

1 Aug 1995   Period start.

3 Sep 1995   Period end.

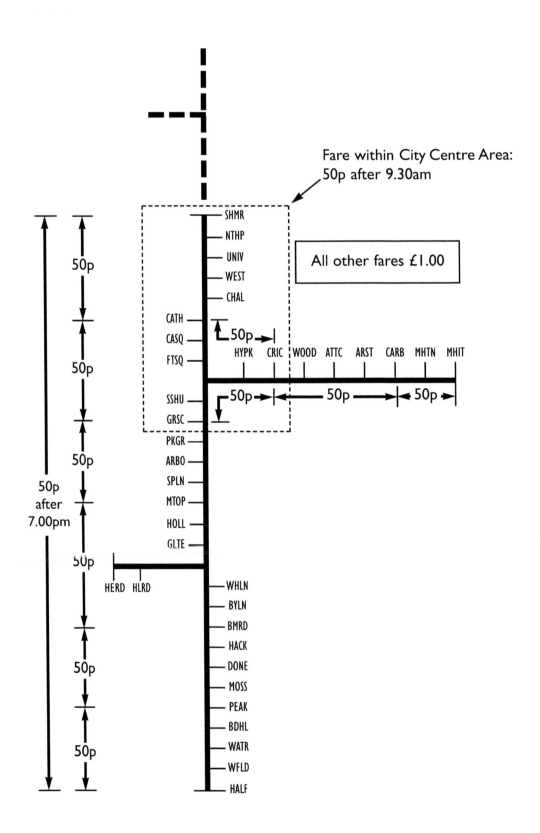

PERIOD 8

Adult Tramstop Prices

4 Sep 1995   Period start.

22 Oct 1995   Period end.

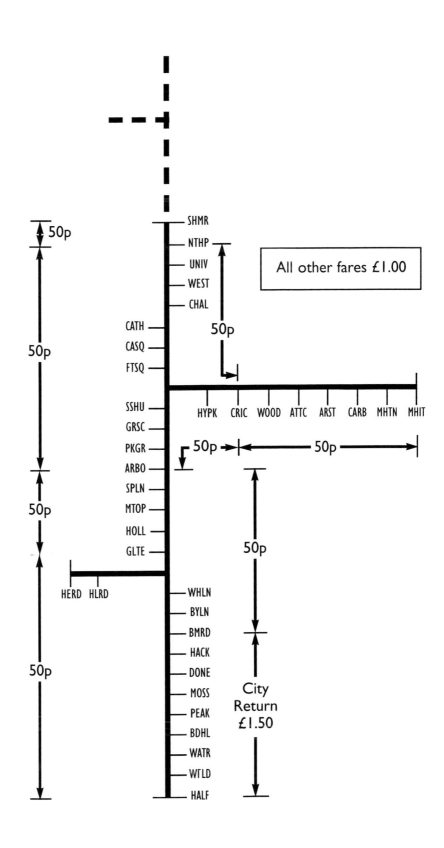

PERIOD 9

Adult Tramstop Prices

26 Oct 1995   First day of fare charging following three days
of free travel with opening of final section, SHA
to MID on 23 Oct 1995.

16 Jun 1996   Period end.

Concessionary fares raised from 15p/25p to 20p/30p
on 3 Mar 1996.

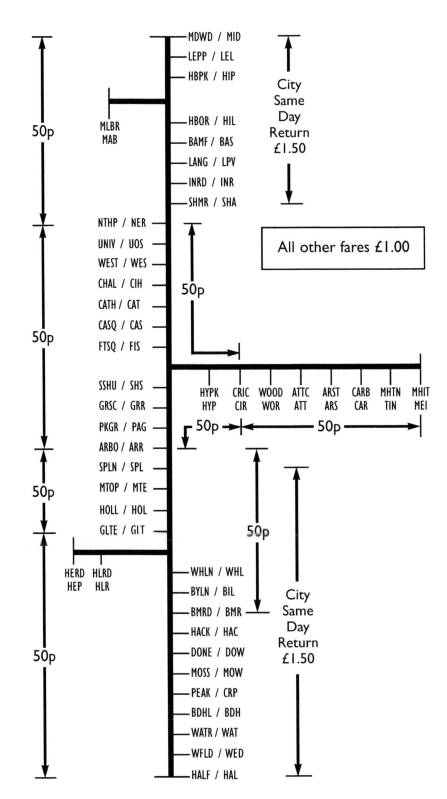

Three-letter tramstop codes
introduced late Feb 1996

PERIOD 10

Adult Tramstop Prices

17 Jun 1996	Introduction of £0.80 City Single fare.
28 Sep 1996	Introduction of £1.50 Student Networker.
1 Apr 1997	Child Fare raised from 20p to 30p.
Jul 1997	Introduction of £1.50 Return for special events.
31 Aug 1997	Period end.

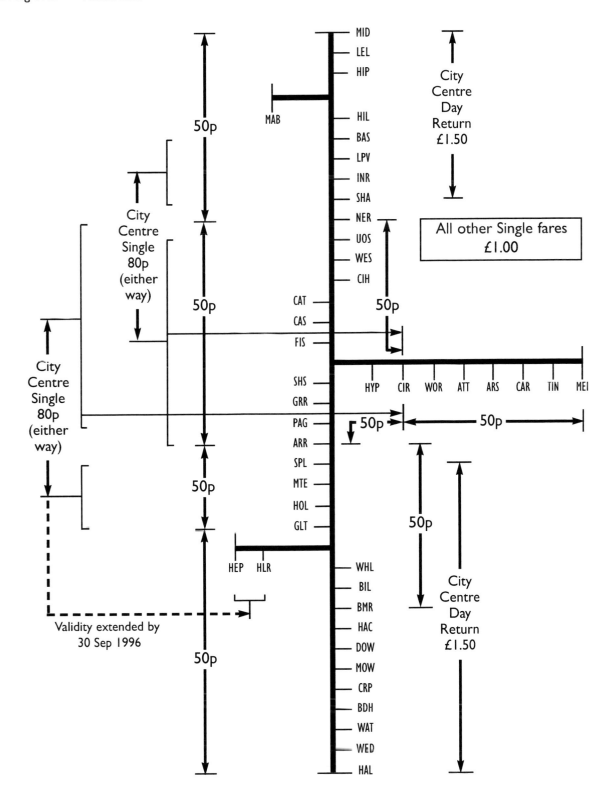

PERIOD 11

Adult Tramstop Prices

1 Sep 1997	General fares increase.
	£2.00 Return introduced.
	Student Networker: £1.80.
	Return (Special Events): £1.50.

17 Nov 1997   £0.60 Child and Senior Citizen Returns introduced.

31 Dec 1997   This structure in place and continuing into 1998.

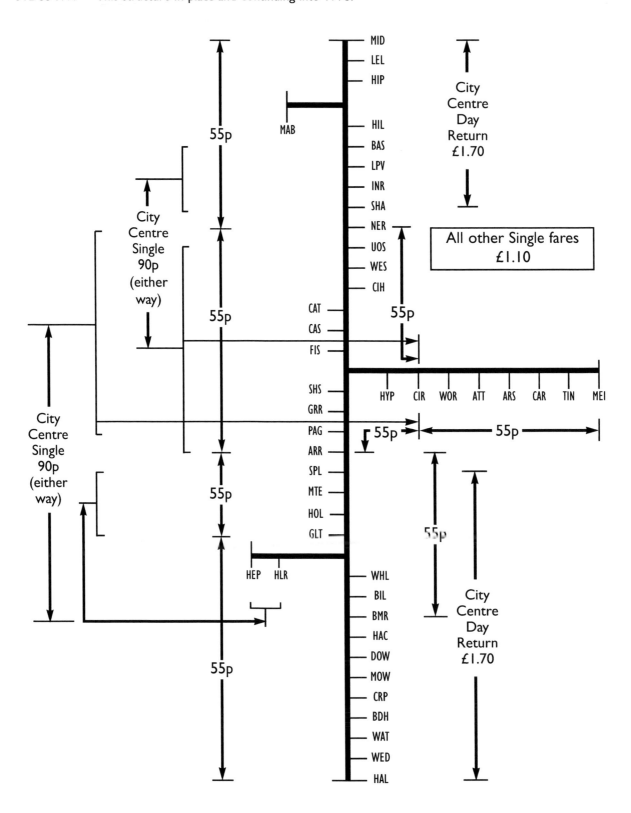

In the tabulations on the following pages, sufficient detail is provided to facilitate identification of the various ticket types. Full details of printing colours are not included.

Summary

Initial designs by BOOTH:
 Types:
 ADC, ABR, BCR.

Initial service issues, mostly by BOOTH:
 Types:
 ACA, BCC, BCMC, CCMC, BCMS, CCMS, BCL, CCML, CCM, DCM, ABW, BCW.

Tramstop vending machine issues by ORION:
 Types:
 DCA, ECA, FCA, GCA, DCC, ECC, FCC;
 3 advertising promotions.

Agents Issues from 22 August 1994 by ORION:
 Types:
 DCSC, ECSC, DCMC, DCSS, ECSS, DCMS, DCSL, DCML, DCMT, DCMF, AACS, DCSA, ECAS, ECAM, ECAF, ECAT, DCAT, DCAF, DCAS, DCW, ECAR, ASPEC, CSPEC, ASDN; two Christmas specials.

Park and Ride card tickets:
 24 varieties.

Other card tickets:
 Networker Travel Cards; VISITOR.

Multi-Pack Cover Cards:
 16 types.

Almex A:
 17 machines noted.

Wayfarer Clipper:
 10 roll types

Other items:
 Unpaid / Penalty Fare Notices; British Rail; Vouchers and coupons; Laminated card for 7 day Networker; Jobseeker; Park and Ride vouchers.

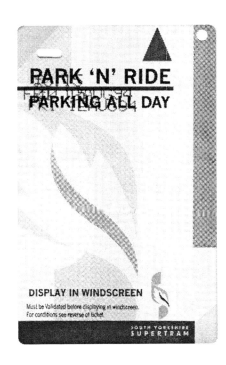

Type ABR
Trial Design.
Not put into service use.

Type ACA
Standard initial style of Tramstop ticket.
Time zero issue! Public operation commenced at 0600hrs, 21 March 1994.

Commemorative special issue
colour - silver-blue

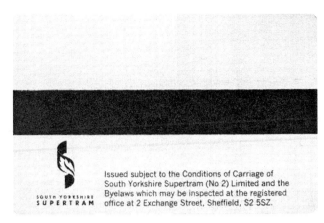

Commemorative special issue
Reverse

Reverse of Type BCC

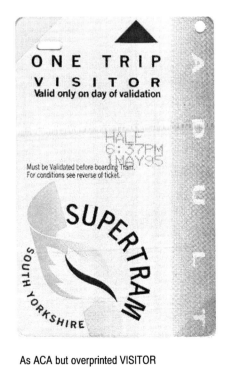

As ACA but overprinted VISITOR

Type BCMS
Standard initial style of Agency ticket.
CCMS, BCMC, CCMC, CCM similar.

INITIAL DESIGNS - Printed by BOOTH - Not put into general service use.

Type	Serial Numbers	Description	Hole?	Slot?	Introduced	Withdrawn	Notes
ADC	eg 000039, 014945	ONE TRIP / ADULT (showing picture of tram)					Existence presumed; no example seen.
		ONE TRIP / CONCESSION (showing picture of tram)					Illustrated in "Supernews" No.2.
		ONE RETURN TRIP / ADULT (showing picture of tram)					
ABR	eg 001634, 01755	PARK 'N' RIDE					
BCR	eg 013112	ONE RETURN TRIP					
	None	ONE RETURN TRIP			Oct 1995		As above but shiny surface. Very limited service use.

INITIAL SERVICE ISSUES - Printed by BOOTH except DCM - Service commenced 21 Mar 1994

Type	Serial Numbers	Description	Hole?	Slot?	Introduced	Withdrawn	Notes
ACA	000001-400000	ONE TRIP / ADULT (2 sizes of serial)	yes	yes	21 Mar 1994		Issued from tramstop vending machines.
ACA	400001-500000	ONE TRIP / ADULT (2 sizes of serial)	yes	yes	21 Mar 1994		Identical to above, but sold generally by agents. Ticket in ACA format.
ACA	none	ONE TRIP / ADULT					Existence suspected. No example seen.
ACA	400451 Reported	ONE TRIP / VIP 22 FEB 1994 / ADULT			22 Feb 1994		
ACA	408311 Seen	ONE TRIP / VIP 27 FEB 1994 / ADULT			27 Feb 1994		
ACA		ONE TRIP / VIP 21 MAR 1994 / ADULT (Opening Day)			21 Mar 1994		
ACA	eg 060421.2	ONE TRIP / VISITOR / ADULT	yes	yes	21 Mar 1994		
BCC	000001-400000	ONE TRIP / CONCESSION (2 sizes of serial)	yes	yes	21 Mar 1994		Issued from tramstop vending machines.
BCMC	051xxx-067xxx	ONE TRIP / MULTI-PACK / CONCESSION / CHILD/SCHOLAR/STUDENT	yes	yes	21 Mar 1994		Issued by agents.
BCMC	075xxx-073xxx	ONE TRIP / MULTI-PACK / CONCESSION / CHILD/SCHOLAR/STUDENT	yes	yes			
BCMC	085xxx-083xxx	ONE TRIP / MULTI-PACK / CONCESSION / CHILD/SCHOLAR/STUDENT	yes	yes			
CCMC	000xxx-039xxx	ONE TRIP / MULTI-PACK / CONCESSION / CHILD/SCHOLAR/STUDENT	yes	yes	early Apr 1994		
CCMC	050xxx-074xxx	ONE TRIP / MULTI-PACK / CONCESSION / CHILD/SCHOLAR/STUDENT	yes	yes			
CCMC	140xxx-177xxx	ONE TRIP / MULTI-PACK / CONCESSION / CHILD/SCHOLAR/STUDENT	yes	yes			
BCMS	080xxx-082xxx	ONE TRIP / MULTI-PACK / CONCESSION / SENIOR CITIZEN / DISABLED	yes	yes	21 Mar 1994		Issued by agents.
BCMS	089xxx-099xxx	ONE TRIP / MULTI-PACK / CONCESSION / SENIOR CITIZEN / DISABLED	yes	yes			
BCMS	130xxx-139xxx	ONE TRIP / MULTI-PACK / CONCESSION / SENIOR CITIZEN / DISABLED	yes	yes			
CCMS	000xxx-030xxx	ONE TRIP / MULTI-PACK / CONCESSION / SENIOR CITIZEN / DISABLED	yes	yes	mid Apr 1994		
BCL	002xxx-003xxx	ONE TRIP / LOCAL	yes	yes	mid Aug 1994		Issued by agents.
BCL	020xxx-021xxx	ONE TRIP / LOCAL	yes	yes	21 Mar 1994		
CCML	000xxx-008xxx	ONE TRIP / LOCAL	yes	yes	mid Apr 1994		
CCM	000xxx- 915xx	ONE TRIP / MULTI-PACK / ADULT	yes	yes	late Apr 1994		Issued by agents.
CCM	none	ONE TRIP / MULTI-PACK / ADULT	yes	yes	21 Mar 1994		Ticket in CCM format. Orion test series.
DCM		ONE TRIP / MULTI-PACK / ADULT	yes	yes	Jul 1994		Issued from tramstop vending machines.
ABW	eg 000226	ONE WEEK / ADULT	yes	yes	21 Mar 1994		Issued by agents
BCW	eg 000404, 000600	ONE WEEK / ADULT	yes	yes			
		COMMEMORATIVE - Launch of Supertram by HRH, The Princess Royal	no	no	23 May 1994		
		Totally blank card	yes	yes			Used for test validations.
		ditto	no	yes			

TRAMSTOP VENDING MACHINE ISSUES - Printed by ORION

Type	Serial Numbers	Description	Hole?	Slot?	Introduced	Withdrawn	Notes
DCA	000001-030000	ONE TRIP / ADULT	no	yes	Nov 1994		
DCA	000004-030000	ONE TRIP / ADULT	no	yes	Nov 1994		Repeat issue due to incorrect manufacture of above.
DCA	030001-700000	ONE TRIP / ADULT	no	yes			
DCA	70001-710000	ONE TRIP / ADULT	yes	yes	mid Jun 1995	Aug 1995	For issue by agents through Wayfarer 3 machines.
DCA	710001-1000000	ONE TRIP / ADULT	no	yes			In DCA format.
DCA	none	ONE TRIP / ADULT					

Type	Serial Numbers	Description	Hole?	Slot?	Introduced	Withdrawn	Notes
ECA	000001-090000	ONE TRIP / ADULT	no	yes	Jul 1995		In DCA format - completely blank reverse.
ECA	090001-310000	ONE TRIP / ADULT	no	no	Aug 1995		Serials repositioned.
ECA	310001-500000	ADULT / VALIDATED	no	no			Serials repositioned.
ECA	500001-710000	ADULT / VALIDATED	no	no			Serials repositioned.
ECA	710001-1000000	ADULT / VALIDATED	no	no			Serials repositioned.
ECA	74xxxx	ADULT / VALIDATED	no	yes			Occasional ticket with slot.
FCA	000001-910000	ADULT / VALIDATED	no	no	Feb 1996		Serial number gap 910001-1000000
GCA	000001-390000	ADULT / VALIDATED	no	no	Sep 1996	1 Jul 1997	
DCC	000001-620000	ONE TRIP / CONCESSION	no	yes	Dec 1994		For issue by agents through Wayfarer 3 machines.
DCC	620001-620000	ONE TRIP / CONCESSION	yes	yes	mid Jun 1995	Aug 1995	As 000001 etc.
DCC	630001-699xxx	ONE TRIP / CONCESSION	no	yes			Serial numbers displaced downwards.
DCC	700001-7098.xx	ONE TRIP / CONCESSION	no	yes			As 630001 etc
DCC	7099xx-730000	ONE TRIP / CONCESSION	no	yes			Serials repositioned.
DCC	730001-820000	ONE TRIP / CONCESSION / VALIDATED	no	yes			
DCC	820001-1000000	ONE TRIP / CONCESSION / VALIDATED	no	yes	Aug 1995		Occasional ticket with slot.
DCC	82xxxx	ONE TRIP / CONCESSION / VALIDATED	no	yes			
ECC	000001-200000	ONE TRIP / CONCESSION / VALIDATED	no	no	mid Nov 1995		Serials repositioned.
ECC	200001-1000000	ONE TRIP / CONCESSION / VALIDATED	no	no			
FCC	000001-189000	ONE TRIP / CONCESSION / VALIDATED	no	no	mid Sep 1996	1 Jul 1997	
	000001-200000	ONE TRIP / ADULT McDonalds promotion - expiry 15.10.95	no	no	21 Aug 1995		"Must be Validated ..." is incorrect. Available at six outlets
	000001-200000	ONE TRIP / CONCESSION McDonalds promotion - expiry 15.10.95	no	no	21 Aug 1995		"Must be Validated ..." is incorrect. Available at six outlets
UCIA	000001-250000	ONE TRIP / ADULT VALIDATED UCI Cinema promotion - expiry 28.3.96	no	no	5 Feb 1996		Available for discounts at Crystal Peaks Cinema.
	000001-200000	ONE TRIP / ADULT VALIDATED McDonalds promotion - expiry 28.04.96	no	no	18 Mar 1996		Available at six outlets
	000001-200000	ONE TRIP / CONCESSION VALIDATED M-Donalds promotion - expiry 28.04.96	no	no	18 Mar 1996		Available at six outlets

AGENTS ISSUES INTRODUCED ON OR AFTER 22 AUG 1994 - printed by ORION

Type	Serial Numbers	Description	Hole?	Slot?	Introduced	Withdrawn	Notes
DCSC	000001-050000	15p / ONE TRIP / CONCESSION	yes	yes	22 Aug 1994		Child fare
DCSC	050001-225000	15p / ONE TRIP / CONCESSION	no	yes	Dec 1994		
DCSC	225001-300000	15p / ONE TRIP / CHILD/SCHOLAR/CONCESSION / ALL FARE STAGES	no	yes	Sep 1995		Triple colour-coded
DCSC	300001-334xxx	15p / SINGLE TRIP / CHILD/SCHOLAR/CONCESSION / SINGLE	no	yes	Dec 1995		Dual colour-coded
ECSC	000001-118xxx	20p / SINGLE TRIP / CHILD/SCHOLAR/CONCESSION / SINGLE	no	no	3 Mar 1996	2 Mar 1996	New single colour design
ECSC	140001-	30p / SINGLE TRIP / CHILD/SCHOLAR/CONCESSION / SINGLE	no	yes	Aug 1997	31 Mar 1997	"30p" overprinted. Square-cut corners. Current as at 31 Dec 1997.
ECSC	160001-	30p / SINGLE TRIP / CHILD/SCHOLAR/CONCESSION / SINGLE	no	yes	1 Apr 1997		"30p" overprinted. Current as at 31 Dec 1997.
DCMC	000001-010000	15p / ONE TRIP / MULTI-PACK/CONCESSION	yes	yes	22 Aug 1994		
DCMC	020001-023xxx	15p / ONE TRIP / MULTI-PACK/CONCESSION	yes	yes	May 1995	Ceased	Note serial number gap.
DCSS	000001-100000	25p / ONE TRIP / CONCESSION	yes	yes	22 Aug 1994		Senior Citizen's fare
DCSS	100001-150000	25p / ONE TRIP / CONCESSION	no	yes	Apr 1995		
DCSS	150001-200000	25p / SENIOR CITIZEN/CONCESSION / ALL FARE STAGES	no	yes	Jun 1995		Triple colour-coded.
DCSS	200001-275000	25p / ONE TRIP / CONCESSION/CONCESSION / ALL FARE STAGES	no	yes	Jul 1995		Triple colour-coded.
DCSS	none	25p / ONE TRIP / CONCESSION/CONCESSION / ALL FARE STAGES	no	no	Dec 1995		As above but no serial number.
DCSS	275001-4369xx	25p / SINGLE TRIP/ CONCESSION/CONCESSION / SINGLE	no	yes	Oct 1995	2 Mar 1996	Dual colour-coded.
ECSS	000001-220000	30p / SINGLE TRIP / SENIOR CITIZEN/MOBILITY / CONCESSION / SINGLE	no	yes	3 Mar 1996		New single colour design. Current at 31 Dec 1997.
ECSS	220001-	30p / SINGLE TRIP / SENIOR CITIZEN/MOBILITY / CONCESSION I SINGLE	no	no	Nov 1997		As above but with square-cut corners. Current at 31 Dec 1997.
DCMS	000001-020000	25p / ONE TRIP I MULTI-PACK / CONCESSION	yes	yes	22Aug 1994		
DCSL	000001-035000	50p / ONE TRIP / LOCAL	yes	yes	late Aug 1994	Ceased	Adult fare - one stage
DCSL	035001-135000	50p / ONE TRIP / ADULT / ONE FARE STAGE	no	yes	Apr 1995		Single colour-coded
DCSL	135001-235000	50p / LOCAL TRIP / ADULT / SINGLE	no	yes	Jan 1996		Single colour-coded
DCSL	235001-	50p / LOCAL TRIP / ADULT / SINGLE	no	yes	Nov 1996		New design and colour change. Current at 31 Dec 1997

Type DCA
Second standard style of Adult tramstop ticket.
(Must be validated .....)

Reverse of Type DCA
".... South Yorkshire Supertram (No.2) Limited ...."

Type FCC
Second standard style of Concession tramstop
ticket, (VALIDATED)

Reverse of Type FCC:
"...South Yorkshire Supertram Limited..."

Colour illustrations on page 26

(1)	Type ADC	- Trial design. Not put into service use.
(2)	Type BCC	- Standard initial style of Concession tramstop ticket. (1st day issue)
(3)	Type DCSS	- Triple colour coded. DCSC similar.
(4)	Type DCMT	Single colour coded. DCSA similar.
(5)	Type DCAT	- Single colour coded. DCAF, DCAS similar.
(6)	Type DCW	- Dual colour coded.
(7)	Bus and Supertram - an unsuccessful venture.
(8)	Type ECSS	- Shaded colour style. ECSC similar.
(9)	Type AACS	- Shaded colour style.

Colour illustrations on page 27

(10)	Type ECAR	- Shaded colour style.
(11)	Type ASDN	- Shaded colour style.
(12)	Christmas Special.
(13)	Type ASPEC	- Special Event.
(14)	Adult Visitor
(15)	Park + Ride	- Initial design - sold at Parkway.
(16)	Park + Ride	- Initial design (Multi-pack) - sold at Parkway
(17)	Park + Ride	- Issued at Middlewood.
(18)	Park + Ride	- Colourful redesign with hologram.

(1)

(2)

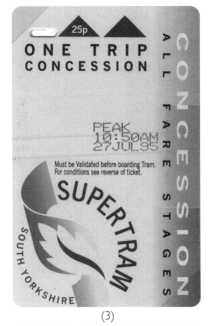

(3)

(4)

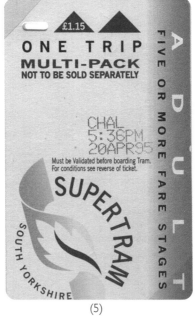

(5)

(6)

(7)

(8)

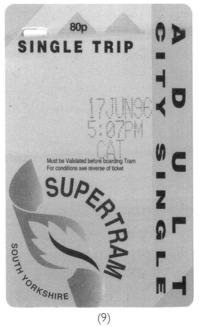

(9)

(10)

(11)

(12)

(13)

(14)

(15)

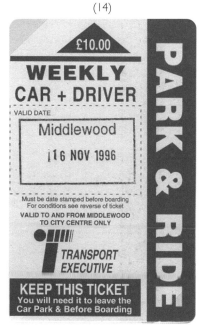

(16)

(17)

(18)

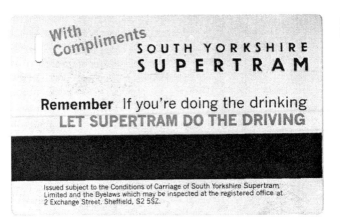

Christmas Special
Reverse.

Type DCSS
Second standard
style of Agency
ticket. DCSC, DCSL,
DCSA similar.

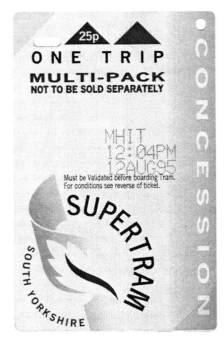

Type DCMS
As DCSS, but for
Multi-Pack Agency
tickets.

Reverse of Type DCSS
showing barcode; "....South Yorkshire Supertram (no.2) Limited ....."

Reverse of Type AACS
showing barcode; "....South Yorkshire Supertram Limited ....."

Type	Serial Numbers	Description	Hole?	Slot?	Introduced	Withdrawn	Notes
DCML	000001-005xxx	50p / ONE TRIP / MULTI-PACK / LOCAL	yes	yes	22 Aug 1994	Ceased	Sold in packs of 10.
DCMT	000001-055000	75p / ONE TRIP / MULTI-PACK / ADULT	yes	yes	22 Aug 1994		
DCMT	055001-100000	75p / ONE TRIP / MULTI-PACK / ADULT	no	yes	Dec 1994		
DCMT	100001-230000	75p / ONE TRIP / MULTI-PACK / ADULT / TWO, THREE & FOUR FARE STAGES	no	yes	Mar 1995	3 Sep 1995	Single colour-coded.
DCMF	000001-075000	80p / ONE TRIP / MULTI-PACK / ADULT	yes	yes	22 Aug 1994	3 Sep 1995	Sold in packs of 5.
DCMF	075001-08Cxxx	80p / ONE TRIP / MULTI-PACK 1 ADULT	no	yes	Jul 1995		
AACS	000001-	80p / SINGLE TRIP / ADULT / CITY SINGLE	yes	yes	17 Jun 1996		Single colour design. Current at 31 Dec 1997.
DCSA	000001-190000	85p / ONE TRIP / ADULT	no	yes	22 Aug 1994		Sold singly.
DCSA	190001-200000	85p / ONE TRIP / ADULT	no	yes	Feb 1995		Barcode on reverse missing.
DCSA	200001-400000	85p / ONE TRIP / ADULT	no	yes	Feb 1995		As above but barcode restored.
DCSA	400001-4278xx	85p / ONE TRIP / ADULT / TWO, THREE & FOUR FARE STAGES	no	yes	Aug 1995	3 Sep 1995	Single colour-coded.
ECAS	000001-390000	90p / SINGLE TRIP / ADULT / SINGLE	no	no	4 Sep 1995		Sold singly. Single colour coded.
ECAS	390001-	£1.00 SINGLE / ADULT	no	no	1 Sep 1997	31 Aug 1997	Front as GCA. Square-cut corners. Current at 31 Dec 1997.
ECAM	000001-100000	£1 / SINGLE TRIP / MULTI-PACK / ADULT / SINGLE (Gaps in serial numbers)	no	yes	4 Sep 1995		Sold in packs of 6 or 13 at discount. Single colour coded.
ECAF	000001-050000	£1 / SINGLE TRIP / MULTI-PACK / ADULT / SINGLE	no	yes	Nov 1995		As above but sold in packs of 6.
ECAF	050001-	£1 / SINGLE TRIP / MULTI-PACK / ADULT / SINGLE	no	yes			Serials repositioned. Current at 31 Dec 1997.
ECAT	000001-050000	£1 / SINGLE TRIP / MULTI-PACK / ADULT / SINGLE	no	yes	Nov 1995		As ECAM/ECAF but sold in packs of 13.
ECAT	050001-	£1 / SINGLE TRIP / MULTI-PACK / ADULT / SINGLE	no	yes			Serials repositioned. Current at 31 Dec 1997.
DCAT	000001-0`2xxx	£1.15 / ONE TRIP / MULTI-PACK / ADULT / FIVE OR MORE FARE STAGES	no	yes	5 Dec 1994	31 Jul 1995	Sold in packs of 10. Single colour coded.
DCAF	000001-007xxx	£1.20 / ONE TRIP / MULTI-PACK / ADULT / FIVE OR MORE FARE STAGES	no	yes	5 Dec 1994	31 Jul 1995	Sold in packs of 5. Single colour coded.
DCAS	000001-010000	£1.30 / ONE TRIP / ADULT / FIVE OR MORE FARE STAGES	no	yes	5 Dec 1994	31 Jul 1995	Sold singly. Barcode omitted. Single colourcoded.
DCAS	010001-027xxx	£1.30 / ONE TRIP / ADULT / FIVE OR MORE FARE STAGES	no	yes	May 1995		As above but with barcode.
DCW	000001-002000	£10 / ONE WEEK / ADULT	yes	yes	22 Aug 1994		Dual colour-coded.
DCW	002001-002500?	£10 / ONE WEEK / ADULT / WEEKLY	no	yes	Oct 1995	28 Jan 1996	As above, but (No.2) removed from conditions.
DCW	?002501-	£10 / ONE WEEK / ADULT / WEEKLY	no	yes	Dec 1995		
	000001-	BUS AND SUPERTRAM / ONE RETURN TRIP / ADULT	no	yes	19 Jun 1995	Ceased	Rotherham to Sheffield City Centre via Meadowhall.
ECAR	000001-	CITY SAME DAY RETURN	no	no	26 Oct 1995		Single colour design. Current at 31 Dec 1997.
ASPEC	000001-C05000	SPECIAL EVENT/ VALIDATED / ADULT / SINGLE	no	no	mid Nov 1995		Square-cut corners.
ASPEC	005001-C15000	SPECIAL EVENT/ VALIDATED / ADULT / SINGLE	no	no	8 Nov 1997		Serials repositioned.
ASPEC	015001-	SPECIAL EVENT/ VALIDATED / ADULT / SINGLE	no	no	mid Nov 1995		Orange serials. Current at 31 Dec 1997.
CSPEC	000001-005000?	ONE TRIP / SPECIAL EVENT / VALIDATED / CONCESSION / SINGLE	no	no			Square-cut corners.
CSPEC	?005001-013xxx	ONE TRIP / SPECIAL EVENT / VALIDATED / CONCESSION / SINGLE	no	yes	mid Nov 1995		Serials repositioned.
ASDN	000001-00000	7 DAY NETWORKER	no	yes	29 Jan 1996	Jun 1996	Single colour design.
ASDN	100001-	7 DAY NETWORKER	no	yes	Nov 1996	Jun 1996	
		FREE / CHRISTMAS SPECIAL / FOR A SAFER HAPPIER FESTIVE SEASON	no	yes	11 Dec 1995	2 Jan 1996	Whiter card. Barcode omitted. Current at 31 Dec 1997.
		FREE / CHRISTMAS SPECIAL / FOR A SAFER HAPPIER FESTIVE SEASON	no	yes	2 Dec 1996	2 Jan 1997	

PARK AND RIDE (CARD TICKETS)

Serial Numbers	Description	Hole?	Slot?	Introduced	Withdrawn	Notes
000001-005xxx(-)	£2.00 (blue)	yes	yes	3 Jan 1995		Reverse 180° out of phase.
005xxx(-)-014xxx+	£2.00 (blue)	no	yes		30 Jun 1995	Above error corrected.
000001 -007xxx+	£2.50 (pink)	no	yes	1 Jul 1995	7 Oct 1995	Square-cut corners.
000001-	£2.50 (blue)	no	no	9 Oct 1995		Rounded corners.
020001-040000	£2.50 (blue)	no	yes	Dec 1995		Whiter card. Serials repositioned.
040001-050000	£2.50 (blue)	no	yes	Jul 1996		Darker card. Ornate serials.
050001-060000	£2.50 (blue)	no	yes	Nov 1996		Reverse reset. Reverse with shiny surface.
060001 -061xxx+	£2.50 (blue)	no	yes	Feb 1997	1 Mar 1997	
000001 -005xxx+	£2.50 / MULTI-PACK (pink)	no	yes	14 Aug 1995	7 Oct 1995	Square-cut corners.
000001-	£2.50 / MULTI-PACK (orange)	no	no	9 Oct 1995		Rounded corners.
010001-022xxx+	£2.50 / MULTI-PACK (orange)	no	yes	Nov 1995	1 Mar 1997	
000001-0015xx+	£10.00 / WEEKLY (green)	no	yes	1 Jul 1995	7 Oct 1995	Square-cut corners.
000001-	£10.00 / WEEKLY (red)	no	no	9 Oct 1995		Rounded corners.
020001-004000	£10.00 / WEEKLY (red)	no	yes	Nov 1995		Whiter card.
040001-006000	£10.00 / WEEKLY (red)	no	yes	May 1996		Darker card.
060001-009000	£10.00 / WEEKLY (red)	no	yes	Oct 1996	1 Mar 1997	
000001-	£2.50 / ONE DAY / MIDDLEWOOD (jade green)	no	no	9 Jun 1996	1 Mar 1997	
000001-	£2.50 / MULTI-PACK / MIDDLEWOOD (jade green)	no	yes	Jul 1996	1 Mar 1997	
000001-	£10.00 / WEEKLY / MIDDLEWOOD (purple)	no	no	9 Jun 1996	1 Mar 1997	
000001-	ONE DAY	no	no	3 Mar 1997		Multi-coloured design. Current at 31 Dec 1997.
000001-	ONE DAY / MULTI-PACK	no	no	3 Mar 1997		Multi-coloured design.
000001-	WEEKLY	no	no	3 Mar 1997		Multi-coloured design. Current at 31 Dec 1997.
000001-	MONTHLY	no	no	3 Mar 1997		Multi-coloured design with hologram. Current at 31 Dec 1997.
None	Car & Driver	n/a	n/a	12 May 1997	29 Mar 1997	Magnetic card.

OTHER CARD TICKETS

Serial Numbers	Description	Hole?	Slot?	Introduced	Withdrawn	Notes
SW000001-	NETWORKER TRAVELCARD - WEEKLY			May 1996		? Current at 31 Dec 1997.
SM000001-	NETWORKER TRAVELCARD - MONTHLY			May 1996		? Current at 31 Dec 1997.
SQ000001-	NETWORKER TRAVELCARD - QUARTERLY			May 1996		? Current at 31 Dec 1997.
	PHOTOCARD to accompany above Travelcards					
000001-	VISITOR / Valid only on day of validation / ADULT VISITOR			by Jul 1996		Current at 31 Dec 1997.

MULTI-PACK COVER CARDS

Associated ticket type	Description	Introduced	Withdrawn	Notes
DCMC	5 PACK / ONE TRIP / CONCESSION / CHILD / SCHOLAR / £0.75	22 Aug 1994		
DCMS	5 PACK / ONE TRIP / CONCESSION / SENIOR CITIZEN / £1.25	22 Aug 1994		
DCML	5 PACK / ONE TRIP / LOCAL / £2.50	22 Aug 1994		
DCMF	5 PACK / ONE TRIP / ADULT / £4.00	22 Aug 1994	3 Sep 1995	
DCMT	10 PACK / ONE TRIP / ADULT / £7.50	Mar 1995	3 Sep 1995	Colour coded.
DCMT	10 PACK / ONE TRIP / ADULT / £7.50 / 2, 3 or 4 Fare Stages	5 Dec 1994	31 Jul 1995	Colour coded.
DCAF	5 PACK / ONE TRIP / ADULT / £6.00 / 5 or more Fare Stages	5 Dec 1994	31 Jul 1995	Colour coded.
DCAT	10 PACK / ONE TRIP / ADULT / £11.50 / 5 or more Fare Stages	4 Sep 1995		Colour coded. Current at 31 Dec 1997.
ECAM then ECAF	BUY 5 GET 1 FREE / ONE TRIP / ADULT / £5.00 / SINGLE TRIPS	4 Sep 1995		Colour coded. Current at 31 Dec 1997.
ECAM then ECAT	BUY 10 GET 3 FREE / ONE TRIP / ADULT / £10.00 / SINGLE TRIPS	1 Sep 1997		Current at 31 Dec 1997.
ECAT	6 PACK / ONE TRIP / ADULT / £5.50 / SINGLE TRIPS	1 Sep 1997		Current at 31 Dec 1997.
ECAT	13 PACK / ONE TRIP / ADULT / £11.00 / SINGLE TRIPS	1 Sep 1997		
PARK AND RIDE	5 PACK / CAR+DRIVER / PARK+RIDE / £11.00 (pink)	14 Aug 1995	7 Oct 1995	
PARK AND RIDE	5 PACK / CAR+DRIVER / PARK+RIDE / £11.00 (orange)	9 Oct 1995	1 Mar 1997	
PARK AND RIDE	MIDDLEWOOD / 5 PACK / £11.00 / CAR+DRIVER / PARK+RIDE	Jul 1996	1 Mar 1997	
PARK AND RIDE	5 PACK / ONE DAY / CAR+DRIVER I PARK+RIDE	3 Mar 1997	29 Mar 1997	Multi-coloured design.

First promotional ticket

Type UCIA - UCI cinema promotion

Type DCSS
Dual colour coded. DCSC was similar.

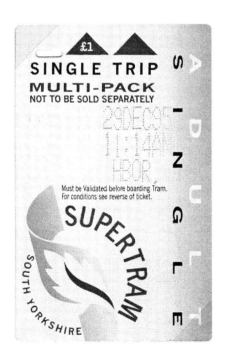

Type ECAT
Single colour coded. ECAF, ECAM similar.

Revised Type ECAS
Introduced with fares increase
on 1 Sep 1997.

Type ASDN reverse
7 Day Networker

Adult Visitor reverse

Multi-pack cover card
Initial design

Multi-pack cover card
Colour coded

Multi-pack cover card
Introduced 1 Sep 1997

Park & Ride - Single
Reverse

Park & Ride - Weekly
Reverse

ALMEX

Machine Number	Description	Introduced	Withdrawn	Notes
0040,0064,0114,0145, 0249,0284,0455,0456, 0465,0480,0483,0487, 1069,3103,6514,7420. 9847	Most machines titled "South Yorkshire P.T.E." Intermittent use of East Midlands Frontrunner rolls. Example of ticket printed on Wayfarer Transit roll known.	12 Oct 1995	16 Jun 1996	Machines loaned by Sheffield Bus Museum.

WAYFARER CLIPPER

Printer / Roll type	Colour	Introduced	Withdrawn	Notes
PLAIN		Feb 1996		
MAINLINE		24 Feb 1996		
WAYFARER TRANSIT		Feb 1996		
SOUTH YORKSHIRE SUPERTRAM	red	Jun 1996		Used very briefly.
SOUTH YORKSHIRE SUPERTRAM	blue	Aug 1996		
THE SUPERTRAM / SIT BACK AND RELAX	red	Dec 1996		For use at special events.
THE SUPERTRAM / SIT BACK AND RELAX	purple	Apr 1997		Current at 31 Dec 1997.
TSB ADVT SAT 12 JULY - SOUTH YORKSHIRE SUPERTRAM	red	end Jun 1997		For use at special events. Current at 31 Dec 1997.
TSB ADVT SAT 12 JULY - THE SUPERTRAM / SIT BACK AND RELAX	purple	end Jun 1997		
SAFE ADVT - THE SUPERTRAM / SIT BACK AND RELAX	purple	4 Sep 1997		

OTHER ITEMS

Ref	Serial numbers	Description	Introduced	Withdrawn	Notes
0538/0494	00001-307xx(+)	UNPAID FARE NOTICE / SOUTH YORKSHIRE SUPERTRAM (No.2) LTD.	1 Apr 1994?		
0538/0794	(-)010xx-031xx(+)	UNPAID FARE NOTICE / SOUTH YORKSHIRE SUPERTRAM LTD.			
0538/0495	(-)040xx-379xx(+)	UNPAID FARE NOTICE / SOUTH YORKSHIRE SUPERTRAM LTD.			
0538/0596	(-)392xx-493xx(+)	UNPAID FARE NOTICE / SOUTH YORKSHIRE SUPERTRAM LTD.			
0578/0795	SY12251,14962 seen	PENALTY FARE NOTICE			
0538/1197	0171 seen	EMERGENCY TICKET / UNPAID PENALTY FARE	Nov 1997		Current at 31 Dec 1997
0538/1197	1181 seen	EMERGENCY TICKET / OR / UNPAID PENALTY FARE	Nov 1997		Current at 31 Dec 1997
		BRITISH RAIL APTIS card showing validity on Supertram			Current at 31 Dec 1997
		BRITISH RAIL SPORTIS ticket showing validity on Supertram			
	00000C1-	CO-OP VOUCHER (Initially valid to 31 Dec 1996)	Apr 1996	31 Oct 1996	
		FREE TRIP COUPON / USE BY 26/04/97	Jan 1997	26 Apr 1997	
		TRAVEL FOR 50p COUPON / USE BY 31ST DECEMBER 1997	mid Nov 1996		
	00001- -038xxx(+)	SUPERTRAM NETWORKER TICKET - Laminated card to hold Wayfarer ticket.	17 Jun 1996	16 Feb 1997	Identical to above but slightly wider
	None	SUPERTRAM NETWORKER TICKET - Laminated card to hold Wayfarer ticket.	17 Feb 1997		Revised design front and reverse with map.
	None	SUPERTRAM NETWORKER TICKET - Laminated card to hold Wayfarer ticket.	Aug 1997		Map revised to show Nunnery Square. Current at 31 Dec 1997.
	00001-	SUPERTRAM NETWORKER TICKET - Laminated card to hold Wayfarer ticket.	15 Sep 1997		
		JOBSEEKER Laminated card			
		£1.00 PARK ONLY (SYPTE)			Pad ticket.
P+R	0001	ONE DAY VOUCHER TO 30TH JUNE 1997	27 May 1997		
P+R		WEEKLY VOUCHER TO 30TH JUNE 1997	27 May 1997		
P+R		MONTHLY VOUCHER TO 30TH JUNE 1997	27 May 1997		
P+R	000001-	5 PACK / ONE DAY / CAR + DRIVER - Booklet of 5 vouchers	1 Jul 1997		Current at 31 Dec 1997

000063

For all your
Bus, Rail and Tram enquiries
CALL TRAVELINE
on
01709 515151

Issued subject to the Conditions of Carriage of South Yorkshire Supertram (No 2)
Limited and the Byelaws which may be inspected at the registered office at
2 Exchange Street, Sheffield, S2 5SZ and the terms and Conditions of the South Yorkshire
Passenger Transport Executive's Park & Ride Scheme.

Park & Ride - Monthly
Reverse

Park & Ride
Standard magnetic card

Park & Ride
Standard magnetic card - Reverse

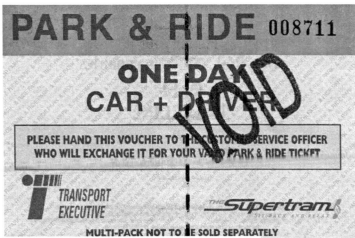

Park & Ride Voucher

For all your
Bus, Rail, and Tram enquiries
CALL
TRAVELINE
on
01709 51 51 51

Issued subject to the Conditions of Carriage of South Yorkshire Supertram (No 2) Limited
and the Byelaws which may be inspected at the registered office at
PO BOX 801, Exchange Street, Sheffield, S2 5YT and the terms and Conditions of the South Yorkshire
Passenger Transport Executive's Park & Ride Scheme.

Reverse

000059

Sheffield Co-operative Society Ltd

- Redeemable in the food and non-food depts, excludes tobacco products
- No change will be given against this voucher
- Can not be used in conjunction with any other coupon or promotion.
- Valid until 31/12/96

£1 VOUCHER

co-op Sheffield

SOUTH YORKSHIRE SUPERTRAM

Sheffield Co-op £1 Voucher

TRAVEL FOR 50p
Mr C Farley
Or Friend
any evening after 7pm
Use by 31st December 1997
(One voucher per person travelling)
Supertram

Travel for 50p Voucher

DOW   No. 08697

SOUTH YORKSHIRE SUPERTRAM LTD.

UNPAID FARE NOTICE

Date of issue: 18·1·96   Time of issue: 08·49

CSA No: 018   Tram No: 13

Recipient Name: ....

Address: ....

....

Post Code: .... Tel No: ....

Amount for which issued: ...25p...........................

Reason for issue TICKET LOST IN MACHINE

Payment to be made to:

SOUTH YORKSHIRE SUPERTRAM LTD.
11 ARUNDEL GATE
SHEFFIELD S2 1PN

0538/0495

Unpaid Fare Notice

Wayfarer - SOUTH YORKSHIRE SUPERTRAM title

Wayfarer - THE Supertram / SIT BACK AND RELAX title

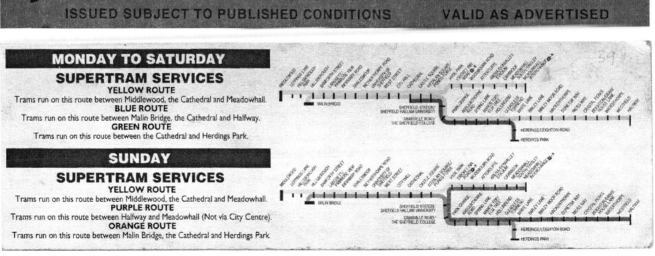

Networker laminated card

1. 21 Mar 1994 to Mid-Jul 1994 (latest noted 14 Jul 1994)
Style: Small and thin. Fare enlarged vertically.

Format	Fare	Class	Ticket Type	Availability	Notes
CLASS	£0.15	CHILD / STUDENT	CONCESSION	Latest example seen 30 Apr 1994.	A
FARE	£0.15	CHILD	CONCESSION	Earliest example seen 3 May 1994.	
TIME	£0.25	SEN CIT / CONC	CONCESSION		
DATE	£0.50	ADULT - LOCAL TRP	ADULT		
TRAMSTOP CODE	£1.00	ADULT - ONE TRIP	ADULT		

Notes:
A   Residual usage of this style noted at WOOD Mar 1995 to May 1995.

2. Mid-Jul 1994 (earliest noted 15-07-94) to Mid 1995.
Style: Small and thin. Fare now normal size.

Format	Fare	Class	Ticket Type	Availability	Notes
FARE	£0.15		CONCESSION		
DATE	£0.25		CONCESSION		
	£0.50		ADULT		
	£1.00		ADULT		
	£1.50		ADULT	Available at some Tramstops commencing 5 Dec 1994.	

3. Mid-Jan 1995 (earliest noted 12 Jan 1995) to late Jul 1995.
Slow transition from style 2 validation. Style: Small and thin.

Format	Fare	Class	Ticket Type	Availability	Notes
FARE	£0.15	CONCESSION			
	£0.25	CONCESSION			
	£0.50	ADULT			
	£1.00	ADULT			
	£1.50	ADULT			

4. Late Jul 1995 to 1 Jul 1997.
Style: Large. Fare, time and tramstop code in bold type.

Format	Fare	Class	Ticket Type	Availability	Notes
FARE	£0.15		CONCESSION	To 2 Mar 1996	B
DATE	£0.20		CONCESSION	From 3 Mar 1996 to 31 Mar 1997	
TIME	£0.25		CONCESSION	To 2 Mar 1996	
TRAMSTOP CODE	£0.30		CONCESSION	From 3 Mar 1996	
CLASS - only for	£0.50		ADULT		
CITY SINGLE	£0.00	CITY CIRCLE	ADULT	From 17 Jun 1996. Certain stops only.	
and CITY RETURN	£1.00		ADULT		
	£1.50		ADULT	To 31 Jul 1996 only.	
	£1.50	CITY RETURN	ADULT	From 4 Sep 1995. Certain stops only. See further notes.	
	£1.50	HWAY - CITY RETURN	ADULT	No Tramstop code. Used initially at LEPP and SPLN.	

Notes:
B   Machines at HBPK, HBOR, HOLL, BYLN, BMRD, PEAK initially programmed without City Return class.

Blue Vending Machine validations are those on the left-hand side of the ticket and those at the centre of the ticket are from the Yellow Validating Machines.

Validation Type 1 : CHILD/STUDENT £0.15
Tramstop : MHIT - Meadowhall Interchange
Ticket Type : BCC

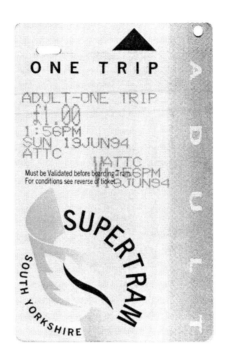

Validation Type 1 : ADULT-ONE TRIP £1.00
Tramstop : ATTC - Attercliffe
Ticket Type : ACA

Validation Type 2 : £0.15
Tramstop : GRSC -
          Granville Road / Sheffield College
Ticket Type : DCC

Validation Type 2 : £0.50
Tramstop : HYPK - Hyde Park
Ticket Type : DCA

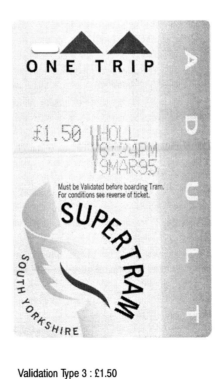

Validation Type 3 : £1.50
Tramstop : HOLL - Hollinsend
Ticket Type : DCA

Validation Type 4 : £1.00
Tramstop : INR - Infirmary Road
Ticket Type : FCA

Validation Type 4 : £0.80 CITY SINGLE
Tramstop : BAS - Bamforth Street
Ticket Type : FCA

Validation Type 4 : £1.50 CITY RETURN
Tramstop : GLT - Gleadless Townend
Ticket Type : GCA

Validation Type 4 : £1.50 HWAY-CITY RETURN
Tramstop : LEPP or SPLN
Ticket Type : ECA

Recreational use of ticket machines on a
sunny Saturday afternoon at West Street
[Dave Aspinwall]

9 - Tramstop Codes - Validations from Blue Vending Machines

NOTES

There have been two distinct printing styles:-
1. Small and thin. In use from 21 Mar 1994 to mid-Jul 1994.
2. Large and bold. In use from late Jul 1995 to 1 Jul 1997.

Earliest and latest known dates of usage are shown.
Number of installed machines shown in Notes.
e.g. 2/1 = 2 Inward / 1 Outward.

Blue ticket vending machine
21 March 1994.

With the third and subsequent
stages of opening, some
machines were supplied or
modified for 6-button operation.
[Dave Aspinwall]

The End:
Ticket validated on final day of operation
of the Abberfield machines at MEI -
Meadowhall Interchange tramstop

Code	From	To	NB	Code	From	To	NB	Notes	Number
MDWD	26-Oct-95	26-Feb-96		MID	29-Feb-96	2-Nov-96		One machine closed 12-Oct-96	2
				MIDI	9-Nov-96	29-Jun-97			
LEPP	26-Oct-95	25-Feb-96		LEL	28-Feb-96	16-Feb-97		Outward machine closed 12-Oct-96	1/1
				LEP	21-Feb-97	13-Apr-97			
				LEL	21-Apr-97	29-Jun-97			
HBPK	26-Oct-95	28-Feb-96		HIP	29-Feb-96	29-Jun-97		Outward machine closed 12-Oct-96	1/1
MLBR	26-Oct-95	28-Feb-96		MAB	29-Feb-96	29-Jun-97		One machine closed 12-Oct-96	2
HBOR	26-Oct-95	28-Feb-96		HIL	29-Feb-96	5-Oct-96		Outward machine closed 12-Oct-96	1/1
				HILI	23-Apr-96	09-Apr-97			
				HIL	9-Apr-97	20-Jun-97			
BAMF	26-Oct-95	28-Feb-96		BAS	29-Feb-96	12-Oct-96		Closed 12-Oct-96	1/1
LANG	26-Oct-95	24-Feb-96		LPV	29-Feb-96	12-Oct-96		Closed 12-Oct-96.	1/1
INRD	26-Oct-95	27-Feb-96		INR	29-Feb-96	12-Oct-96		Closed 12-Oct-96.	1/1
SHMR	29-Jul-95	24-Feb-96		SHA	29-Feb-96	12-Oct-96		Closed 13-Oct-96.	1/1

Validation type : small and thin
4 letter Tramstop code :
    CARB - Carbrook
Ticket Type : ACA

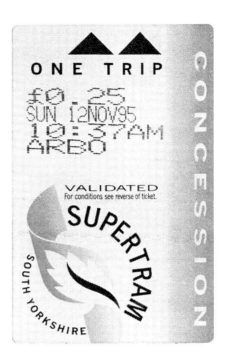

Validation type : large and bold
4 letter Tramstop code :
    ARBO - Arbouthorne Road
Ticket Type: DCC

Validation type : large and bold
4 letter Tramstop code + ■
    BYLN - Birley Lane
Ticket Type : DCA

Validation type : large and bold:
Tramstop :
    WATERTH (an oddity) - Waterthorpe
Ticket Type : promotional

Validation type : large and bold:
3 letter Tramstop code :
    MTE - Manor Top / Elm Tree
Ticket Type : FCA

Validation type : large and bold
3 letter Tramstop code : + "l":
    MIDI - Middlewood
Ticket Type: FCC

Code	From	To	NB	Code	From	To	NB	Notes	Number
NTHP	29-Jul-95	29-Feb-96		NER	29-Feb-96	12-Oct-96		Closed 13-Oct-96.	1/1
UNIV	29-Jul-95	29-Feb-96		UOS	29-Feb-96	30-Jun-97			2/1
WEST WEST■	2-Aug-95 29-Jul-95	24-Feb-96 24-Aug-95		WES	29-Feb-96	29-Jun-97		Two machines closed 13-Oct-96.	2/2
CHAL CHALL	29-Jul-95 18-Aug-95	27-Feb-96 24-Feb-96		CIH	28-Feb-96	29-Jun-97		Four machines closed 13-Oct-96.	3/3
CATH CA	29-Jul-95 1-Aug-95	28-Feb-96 4-Sep-95		CAT AT	28-Feb-96	30-Jun-97	 A	A. Known only on 6-Dec-96 and 25-Apr-97.	3/3
CASQ	29-Jul-95	7-Mar-96		CAS CASI	28-Feb-96 16-Mar-96	1-Jul-97 26-Nov-96			2/2
FTSQ FTSQY	21-Mar-94 29-Sep-95 29-Jul-95	14-Jul-94 28-Feb-96 05-Sep-95		FIS	27-Feb-96	30-Jun-97			4/- 3/- 3/3
HYPK	21-Mar-94 28-Jul-95	29-Jun-94 29-Feb-96		HYP	1-Mar-96	17-Aug-96		Closed Aug-96.	2/2
CRIC CRICK	11-Jun-94 28-Jul-95 21-Mar-94 28-Jul-95	19-Jun-94 01-Mar-96 29-Jun-94 04-Nov-95		CIR	1-Mar-96	30-Jun-97		One machine closed by Sep-96.	2/2 1/2
WOOD	21-Mar-94 28-Jul-95	14-Jul-94 29-Feb-96	B	WOR WORI	3-Mar-96 19-Apr-96	9-Sep-96 15-May-96		Closed by 12-Sep-96. B: First validation style also known to have been used 17-Mar-95 to 27-May-95.	2/2
ATTC	21-Mar-94 28-Jul-95	14-Jul-94 1-Mar-96		ATT	1-Mar-96	13-Sep-96		Closed by 14-Sep-96.	2/2
ARST	28-Jul-95	29-Feb-96		ARS	2-Mar-96	11-Sep-96		Closed by 14-Sep-96.	2/2
CARB	21-Mar-94 28-Jul-95	28-Jun-94 29-Feb-96		CAR	1-Mar-96	12-Sep-96		Closed by 12-Sep-96.	2/2
MHTN	21-Mar-94 28-Jul-95	10 Jul 04 29-Feb-96		TIN	29-Feb-96	10-Sep-96		By 12-Sep-96.	2/2
MHIT	21-Mar-94 28-Jul-95	12-Jul-94 29-Feb-96		MEI MEII	29-Feb-96 21-May-96	1-Jul-97 1-Jul-97			2 3
SSHU	8-Jul-95	1-Mar-96		SHS	1-Mar-96	17-Sep-96		Closed by 18-Sep-96.	2/2
GRSC	28-Jul-95	1-Mar-96		GRR	1-Mar-96	29-Jun-96		Closed 30-Jun-96.	2/2
PKGR	28-Jul-95	29-Feb-96		PAG	1-Mar-96	29-Jun-96		Closed 30-Jun-96.	2/2
ARBO	28-Jul-95	1-Mar-96		ARR	1-Mar-96	29-Jun-96		Closed 30-Jun-96.	2/2
SPLN	28-Jul-95	1-Mar-96		SPL	1-Mar-96	29-Jun-96		Closed 30-Jun-96.	2/2

Code	From	To	NB	Code	From	To	NB	Notes	Number
MTOP **MTOP■**	27-Jul-95 28-Jul-95	1-Mar-96 29-Sep-95		**MTE**	1-Mar-96	29-Jun-97		Four machines closed 19-Sep-96.	3/3
HOLL	27-Jul-95	1-Mar-96		**HOL**	1-Mar-96	18-Sep-96		Closed 18-Sep-96.	1/1
GLTE **GLTE ■**	27-Jul-95 31-Jul-95	1-Mar-96 15-Sep-95		**GLT**	1-Mar-96	29-Jun-97		Two machines. Closed by 18-Sep-96.	3/2
HLRD	30-Jan-96	1-Mar-96		**HLR**	6-Mar-96	28-Jun-96		Closed 30-Jun-96 .	1/1
(HERD)								Validation may exist. Machines vandalised from start.	2
WHLN	27-Jul-95	1-Mar-96		**WHL**	1-Mar-96	14-Sep-96		Closed by 18-Sep-96.	1/1
BYLN **BYLN ■**	30-Jul-95 27-Jul-95	18-Nov-95 21-Sep-95						Closed Nov-95.	1/1
BMRD	27-Jul-95	18-Nov-95						Closed Nov-95.	1/1
HACK	28-Jul-95	18-Nov-95						Closed Nov-95	1/1
DONE **DONE■**	27-Jul-95 28-Jul-95	11-Sep-95 21-Sep-95						Closed Nov-95	1/1
MOSS	27-Jul-95	16-Nov-95						Closed Nov-95.	1/1
PEAK **PEAK■**	27-Jul-95 27-Jul-95	18-Nov-95 13-Sep-95						Closed Nov-95	3/1
BDHL	27-Jul-95	20-Nov-95						Closed Nov-95.	1/1
WATR **WATERTH**	27-Jul-95 27-Jul-95	18-Nov-95 2-Oct-95						Closed Nov-95	1/1
WFLD	27-Jul-95	18-Nov-95						Closed Nov-95.	1/1
HALF	28-Jul-95	19-Nov-95						Closed Nov-95.	2

Supertrams 25 and 03
at Shalesmoor, 23 October 1995.
[Dave Aspinwall]

NOTES

There have been three styles of validation:-
1. **"V"** = With "V" and tramstop code at top of printed data.
2. **"noV"** = Without "V" and tramstop code at top of printed data.
3. **"Inv"** = Inverted with tramstop code at bottom of printed data and no "V".

Change from 4-letter code to 3-letter code occurred at end of Feb 1996. Earliest and latest known dates of usage of validation styles are shown. Number of installed machines shown below code.
e.g. 2/1 = 2 Inward / 1 Outward

Must be Validated before boarding Tram.
For conditions see reverse of ticket.

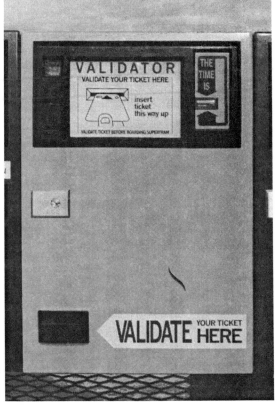

Yellow validating machine
21 March 1994.
[Dave Aspinwall]

Manually-validated ticket:
(this was common practice)
Tramstop: CAT - Cathedral

Code	V	noV	Inv	From	To	NB	Code	V	noV	Inv	From	To	NB	Notes
MDWD 2	✓			26-Oct-95	27-Nov-95		**MID**							One machine closed mid-Nov 1996.
		✓		26-Oct-95	4-Nov-95									
			✓	4-Dec-95	27-Feb-96					✓	1-Mar-96	29-Jun-97		
I FPP 1/1		✓		26-Oct-95	21-Dec-95		**LEL**							Outward machine closed mid-Nov 1996.
			✓	4-Dec-95	28-Feb-96					✓	29-Feb-96	29-Jun-97		
HBPK 1/1		✓		26-Oct-95	only		**HIP**							Outward machine closed mid-Nov 1996.
			✓	26-Oct-95	28-Feb-96					✓	29-Feb-96	29-Jun-97		
MLBR 2		✓		26-Oct-95	4-Nov-95		**MAB**							One machine closed mid-Nov 1996.
			✓	26-Oct-95	24-Feb-96					✓	29-Feb-96	30-Jun-97		
HBOR 1/1	✓			26-Oct--95	5-Nov-95		**HIL**							Outward machine closed mid-Nov 1996.
			✓	26-Oct-95	28-Feb-96					✓	29-Feb-96	29-Jun-97		
BAMF 1/1	✓			26-Oct-95	only		**BAS**							
		✓		26-Oct-95	18-Nov-95									
			✓	9-Dec-95	18-Feb--96					✓	29-Feb-96	29-Jun-97		

Code	V	noV	Inv	From	To	NB	Code	V	noV	Inv	From	To	NB	Notes
LANG 1/1		✓		26-Oct-95	only		**LPV**								
			✓	26-Oct-95	22-Feb-96					✓	29-Feb-96	30-Jun-97		
INRD 1/1	✓			26-Oct-95	18-Nov-95		**INR**								
			✓	4-Dec-95	15-Feb-96					✓	29-Feb-96	29-Jun-97		
SHMR 1/1	✓			20-Oct-95	xx-Nov-95		**SHA**								
		✓		27-Feb-95	13-Oct-95										
			✓	7-Dec-95	28-Feb-96					✓	29-Feb-96	29-Jun-97		
NTHP 1/1	✓			27-Feb-95	5-Dec-95		**NER**								
		✓		27-Feb-95	3-Nov-95										
			✓	16-Dec-95	29-Feb-96					✓	29-Feb-96	29-Jun-97		
UNIV 2/1	✓			27-Feb-95	8-Dec-95		**UOS**								
		✓		27-Feb-95	11-Dec-95										
			✓	14-Dec-95	28-Feb-96					✓	29-Feb-96	1-Jul-97		
WEST 2/2	✓			27-Feb-95	9-Dec-95		**WES**							Two machines closed mid-Nov 1996.
		✓		27-Feb-95	23-Feb-96				✓		2-Mar-96	26-Apr-96		
			✓	21-Dec-95	28-Feb-96					✓	29-Feb-96	30-Jun-97		
W	✓			16-Mar-95	20-Apr-95		**WE**			✓	26-Apr-96	29-May-96		
CHAL 3/3	✓			21-Sep-95	14-Feb-96		**CIH**	✓			1-Mar-96	2-Apr-96		Four machines closed by 2-Nov-96.
		✓		27-Feb-95	15-Feb-96				✓		29-Feb-96	3-Apr-96		
			✓	16-Dec-95	28-Feb-96					✓	29-Feb-96	1-Jul-97		
CATH 3/3	✓			18-Feb-95	14-Feb-96		**CAT**								
		✓		18-Feb-95	15-Feb-96										
			✓	29-Sep-95	28-Feb-96					✓	29-Feb-96	1-Jul-97		
CASQ 2/2	✓			18-Feb-95	22-Feb-96		**CAS**	✓			1-Mar-96	27-Mar-96		
		✓		18-Feb-95	8-Dec-95										
			✓	29-Sep-95	28-Feb-96					✓	27-Feb-96	1-Jul-97		
FTSQ 2/- 3/- 3/3	✓			21-Mar-94	19-Sep-95	B	**FIS**							B: One machine printing extra data line of 12 digits 4-Aug-95 to 24-Sep-95.
		✓		10-Dec-94	23-Sep-95										
			✓	25-Sep-95	28-Feb-96					✓	27-Feb-96	1-Jul-97		
HYPK 1/1	✓			21-Mar-94	24-Feb-96		**HYP**								
		✓		18-Aug-95	28-Jan-96										
			✓	24-Feb-96	only					✓	2-Mar-96	29-Jun-97		
CRIC 1/1 2/1	✓			15-Dec-94	15-Feb-96		**CIR**								
			✓	5-Dec-95	1-Mar-96					✓	1-Mar-96	1-Jul-97		
CRICK	✓			21-Mar-94	4-Nov-95										
		✓		18-Jul-95	23-Aug-95										
WOOD 1/1	✓			21-Mar-94	17-Feb-96		**WOR**	✓			1-Mar-96	23-Apr-96		
										✓	12-Apr-96	29-Jun-97		
ATTC 1/1	✓			21-Mar-94	15-Feb-96	C	**ATT**	✓			4-Mar-96	only		C: Gap late Sep-95 to early Jan-96.
		✓		25-Jan-95	11-Jan-96										
			✓	4-Feb-96	28-Feb-96					✓	1-Mar-96	29-Jun-97		
ARST 1/1	✓			22-Aug-94	29-Feb-96		**ARS**	✓			7-Mar-96	20-Apr-96		
		✓		18-Dec-94	9-Feb-96				✓		23-Mar-96	30-Mar-96		
										✓	27-Apr-96	29-Jun-97		
							ARSO			✓	30-Nov-96	5-Dec-96		

Code	V	noV	Inv	From	To	NB	Code	V	noV	Inv	From	To	NB	Notes
CARB 1/1	✓			21-Mar-94	29-Feb-96		**CAR**	✓			29-Feb-96	22-Mar-96		
										✓	27-Mar-96	30-Jun-97		
MHTN 1/1	✓			21-Mar-94	29-Feb-96		**TIN**	✓			1-Mar-96	24-Jul-96		Outward machine closed by 1-Nov-96.
										✓	27-Mar-96	20-Jun-97		
MHIT 4	✓			21-Mar-94	8-Dec-95		**MEI**							
3		✓		30-Dec-94	9-Dec-95										
			✓	9-Nov-95	29-Feb-96					✓	1-Mar-96	1-Jul-97		
SSHU 1/1	✓			22-Aug-94	3-Nov-95		**SHS**							
		✓		5-May-95	21-Feb-96				✓		5-Mar-96	27-Mar-96		
			✓	15-Dec-95	24-Feb-96					✓	1-Mar-96	29-Jun-97		
GRSC 1/1	✓			22-Aug-94	14-Jan-96		**GRR**							
		✓		1-Mar-95	13-Jan-96										
			✓	18-Jan-96	29-Feb-96					✓	1-Mar-96	29-Jun-97		
PKGR 1/1	✓			22-Aug-94	3-Nov-95		**PAG**							
		✓		18-Feb-95	13-Jan-96										
			✓	17-Nov-95	29-Feb-96					✓	1-Mar-96	29-Jun-97		
ARBO 1/1	✓			22-Aug-94	16-Jun-95		**ARR**							
		✓		21-Jan-95	9-Dec-95										
			✓	4-Jan-96	1-Mar-96					✓	1-Mar-96	29-Jun-97		
SPLN 1/1	✓			22-Aug-94	14-Jan-95		**SPL**							A: Earliest use of "noV" format. Gap in usage Dec-94
		✓		22-Nov-94	6-Jan-96	A								
			✓	3-Jan-96	29-Feb-96					✓	1-Mar-96	18-Jun-97		
MTOP 3/3	✓			5-Dec-94	12-Jan-96		**MTE**	✓			7-Mar-96	17-Jun-96		Four machines closed by mid Nov-96.
		✓		5-Dec-94	1-Mar-96				✓		5-Mar-96	25-Jun-96		
			✓	19-Dec-95	29-Feb-96					✓	1-Mar-96	1-Jul-97		
HOLL 1/1	✓			16-Jan-95	8-Dec-95		**HOL**							B: Gap late Dec-94 to mid Mar-95.
		✓		5-Dec-94	7-Dec-95	B								
			✓	7-Dec-95	1-Mar-96					✓	2-Mar-96	29-Jun-97		
GLTE 3/2	✓			5-Jan-95	1-Mar-96		**GLT**	✓			2-Mar-96	12-Jul-96		Two machines closed by mid Nov-96.
		✓		5-Dec-94	3-Feb-96									
			✓	17-Dec-95	1-Mar-96					✓	2-Mar-96	29-Jun-97		
							Ø			✓	14-Jun-96	30-Jun-97		Symbol instead of code.
HLRD 1/1	✓			3-Apr-95	3-Oct-95		**HLR**							Outward machine closed by end Nov-96.
		✓		3-Apr-95	23-Dec-95									
			✓	30-Dec-95	28-Feb-96					✓	4-Mar-96	29-Jun-97		
HERD 2	✓			12-May-95	17-Feb-96	C	**HEP**							C: Gap Aug-95 to Dec-95.
		✓		3-Apr-95	9-Dec-95										D: Both machines closed/vandalised by end Nov-96.
			✓	29-Feb-96	only					✓	2-Mar-96	17-Oct-96	D	
WHLN 1/1		✓		27-Mar-95	29-Feb-96		**WHL**		✓		2-Mar-96	4-May-96		
			✓	8-Dec-95	28-Feb-96					✓	1-Mar-96	1-Jul-97		
BYLN 1/1	✓			18-Apr-95	15-Sep-95		**BIL**							
		✓		27-Mar-95	29-Feb-96					✓	6-Mar-96	24-Apr-96		
			✓	8-Dec-95	17-Feb-96					✓	8-Mar-96	29-Jun-97		
BMRD 1/1	✓			15-Jun-95	29-Feb-96		**BMR**	✓			2-Mar-96	16-Apr-96		
		✓		27-Mar-95	17-Feb-96				✓		2-Mar-96	26-Apr-96		
										✓	11-May-96	29-Jun-97		

Code	V	noV	Inv	From	To	NB	Code	V	noV	Inv	From	To	NB	Notes
HACK 1/1	✓	✓	✓	27-Mar-95 31-Jul-95 10-Feb-96	13-Sep-95 3-Feb-96 26-Feb-96		HAC		✓		2-Mar-96	29-Jun-97		
DONE 1/1		✓	✓	27-Mar-95 17-Jan-96	12-Jan-96 2-Mar-96		DOW		✓		2-Mar-96	29-Jun-97		
MOSS 1/1	✓	✓		27-Mar-95 17-Jan-96	25-Feb-96 2-Mar-96	E	MOW	✓	✓	✓	8-Mar-96 8-Mar-96 28-Jul-96	29-Jun-96 29-Jun-96 29-Jun-97		E: Possible gap Apr to Nov-95.
PEAK 3/1	✓	✓	✓	27-Mar-95 27-Mar-95 11-Oct-95	1-Mar-96 29-Feb-96 1-Mar-96		CRP	✓	✓	✓	2-Mar-96 2-Mar-96 5-Mar-96	29-Mar-96 28-Mar-96 29-Jun-97		Two inward machines closed by 26-Oct-96.
BDHL 1/1	✓	✓		29-Mar-95 27-Mar-95	9-Feb-96 17-Feb-96		BDH BDHO	✓	✓ ✓		4-Mar-96 26-Mar-96 11-Mar-96	7-Mar-96 20-Jun-97 13-Jul-96		
WATR 1/1 ATR		✓ ✓	✓	27-Mar-95 30-Dec-95 2-May-95	1-Mar-96 25-Feb-96 25-May-95		WAT		✓ ✓		2-Mar-96 27-Apr-96	18-Apr-96 22-May-97		Outward machine closed by 26-Oct-96.
WFLD 1/1	✓	✓	✓	22-Apr-95 27-Mar-95 20-Dec-95	15-Nov-95 15-Feb-96 1-Mar-96	A	WED		✓ ✓		8-Mar-96 29-Mar-96	29-Jun-96 29-Jun-97		A: Possible gaps. Outward machine closed by 26-Oct-96.
HALF 2		✓		27-Mar-95	25-Feb-96		HAL		✓ ✓		2-Mar-96 20-Jul-96	11-Jul-96 30-Jun-97		One machine closed by 26-Oct-96.

4 LETTER CODES

Validation type : V
Tramstop : SSHU
    - Sheffield University /Hallam University
Ticket Type : DCMT

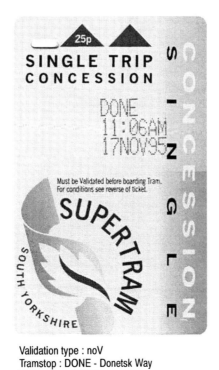

Validation type : noV
Tramstop : DONE - Donetsk Way
Ticket Type : DCSS

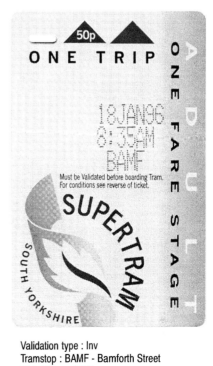

Validation type : Inv
Tramstop : BAMF - Bamforth Street
Ticket Type : DCSL

4 LETTER CODES

3 LETTER CODES

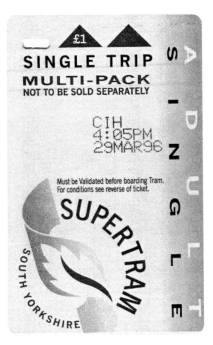

Validation type : V with 12-digit serial
Tramstop : FTSQ - Fitzalan Square
Ticket Type : DCSL

Validation type : V
Tramstop : TIN - Meadowhall South / Tinsley
Ticket Type : ECAT

Validation type : noV
Tramstop : CIH - City Hall
Ticket Type : ECAF

3 LETTER CODES

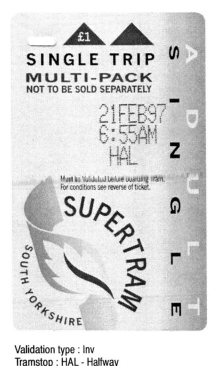

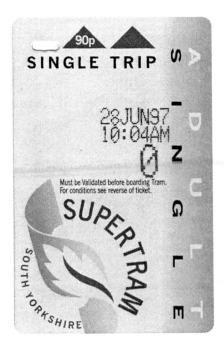

Validation type : Inv
Tramstop : HAL - Halfway
Ticket Type : ECAF

Oddities:
Tramstop : ARS +"O" - Arena / Sheffield Stadium
Ticket Type : ECSC

Tramstop : Ø - Gleadless Townend
Ticket Type : ECAS

11 - Validation Styles from Wayfarer 3 Machines

STYLE 1 - Mar 1994 and Aug 1994

Format A	Format B	Format C
CLASS	CLASS	CLASS
FARE	FARE	FARE
DATE	DATE	DATE
NUMBER	TIME	TIME
TIME	NUMBER	NUMBER
		NUMBER

Fare	Class	Format	Dates noted in use	Ticket type
£0.15	CHILD / STUDENT	A	06-Aug-94 to 20-Aug-94	CCMC
£0.25	SEN CIT / CONCESSION	B	06-Aug-94 to 20-Aug-94	BCMS
£0.50	ADULT - LOCAL TRIP	B	06-Aug-94 to 20-Aug-94	BCL
£0.75	ADULT - ONE TRIP	B	06-Aug-94 to 20-Aug-94	CCM
£10.00	ADULT - 1 WEEK	C	10-Mar-94	ABW, BCW

Note: Weekly tickets pre-validated prior to opening of first stage.

Format A
CHILD STUDENT £0.15
Ticket Type : CCMC

Format B
ADULT - LOCAL TRIP £0.50
Ticket Type : BCL

Format C
ADULT WEEK £10.00
Ticket Type : BCW

STYLE 2 - 20 Aug 1994 to May 1995

Format	Fare	Ticket Type		Machine	Agent	Location	Dates noted in use
FARE M/C NO.	£0.15	BCC	DCSC*	4905	0669		27-Feb-95 to 24-Mar-95
DATE TIME	£0.25	BCC	DCSS	5215	1986		7-Dec-94 to 23-Dec-94
AGENT No.	£0.50	BCL	DCSL†	5278	1986		5-Dec-94 to 9-Dec-94
	£0.85	ACA	DCSA	8000	8000		(reported - not seen)
	£10.00	BCW	DCW	8003	8000		2-Feb-95
				8006	8000		3-Feb-95 to 17-Apr-95
	* also DCSS			9002	1986	Exchange Street	27-Aug-94 to 10-Mar-95
	† also DCML			9003	1986	Pinstone Street	22-Aug-94 to 25-Apr-95
				9004	1986	Sheffield Interchange	23-Aug-94 to 13-Apr-95
				9005	1986	Meadowhall	20-Aug-94 to 18-Dec-94
				9008	1986	Rotherham	23-Aug-94 to 28-Jan-95
				9022	1986		24-Mar-95 to 10-May-95
				9033	1986		22-Mar-95 to 20-Mar-95
				9044	1986		3-Feb-95
				9987	9999		19-Oct-94 to 26-Jan-95
				9992	9998		21-Feb-95
				9993	9998		13-Nov-94 to 9-Dec-94
				9999	9999	United News, Arbourthorne Road	3-Dec-94 to 5-Dec-94

£0.85
Ticket Type : DCSA

STYLE 3 - Early Jun 1995 to late Aug 1995

Format	Fare	Ticket type	Machine	Agent	Location	Dates noted in use
DATE-TIME-M/C No.-AGENT No.	£0.15	DCC62xxxxx	4923	9998		29-Jun-95 to 23-Aug-95
FARE	£0.25	DCC62xxxxx	4931	1986	Pinstone Street	03-Jun-95 to 18-Aug-95
	£0.50	DCA70xxxxx*	4943	1986	Sheffield Interchange	17-Jun-95 to 24-Aug-95
	£0.85	DCA70xxxxx	5231	8000	Manor Top	15-Jun-95 to 24-Aug-95
	£1.30†	DCA70xxxxx	5236	1986	Exchange Street	10-Jun-95 to 22-Aug-95
	£10.00	DCA70xxxxx				

* also BCL
† data in Style 2 format

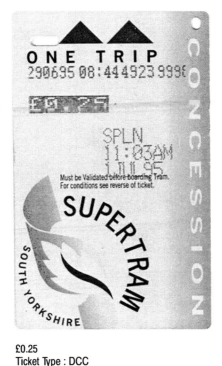

£0.25
Ticket Type : DCC

£1.30
Ticket Type : DCA

Wayfarer 3 Datasheet - [1]

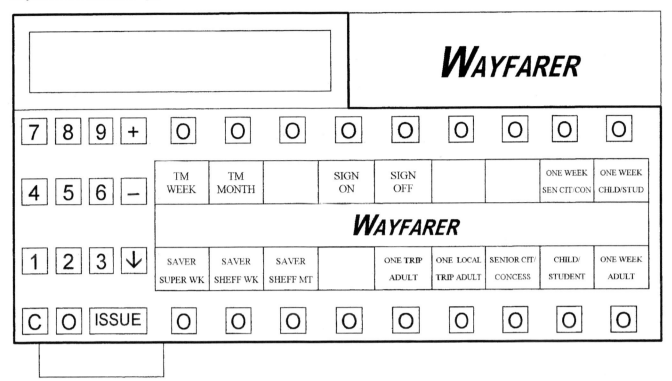

DETAILS:

Date seen: Early August 1994 at South Yorkshire Passenger Transport Executive's Exchange Street Travel Shop.

Model: Model 13392 / serial no 005206*. A special model to meet Supertram's requirements. Grey casing. There is an extra display unit fitted to the top of the machine. This read "Select Card / Travelmaster"- The slot on the left side of the machine, normally used for ticket issue, was blanked off. Slot provided on right (? almost certain) side of machine for inserting cards.

Keyboard: Two buttons, top row, right hand end and five buttons, bottom row, right hand end all with purple background and intended for Supertram use although there were no tickets in use that corresponded with the two top row buttons. Annotated buttons at left hand end of top and bottom rows intended for SYPTE but not in use.

Wayfarer 3 Datasheet - [2]

■■■□□□□□□□□ 14 : 58
Idle 20.AUG.94

WAYFARER

| 7 | 8 | 9 | + | O | O | O | O | O | O | O | O | O |

| | | | | | | | SIGN ON | SIGN OFF | | | DAY TM TODAY | DAY TM TOMORROW |
| 4 | 5 | 6 | − | | | | | | | | | |

WAYFARER

| | | | | | | | ONE TRIP ADULT | ONE LOCAL TRIP ADULT | SENIOR CIT/ CONCESS | CHILD/ STUDENT | ONE WEEK ADULT |
| 1 | 2 | 3 | ↓ | | | | | | | | |

| C | O | ISSUE | O | O | O | O | O | O | O | O | O |

DETAILS:

Date seen: 20 August 1994 at South Yorkshire Passenger Transport Executive's Exchange Street Travel Shop.

Model: Model 13392 / serial no 005220*. Refer to datasheet [1] for general details.

Keyboard: Annotated buttons at right hand end of top row intended for SYPTE use but not commissioned. The machine had just been reprogrammed ready for putting into use on Monday 22 August 1994.

Display: Note the eleven "milk bottles" - indicating that the machine's memory is 3/11ths full. The machine can operate without a module inserted. However data is downloaded intermittently via a module.

Waybill: Card type Waybill (same size as magnetic card):

Close Down Waybill	
Agent no.	: 1686
Machine no	: 9002
Start up	: 19AUG94 15:35
Close down	: 19AUG94 15:35
Tickets	: 1
Total Cash	: £0.85
Commission	: £0.04

Other Publications

London Transport Numerical Stage Punch Tickets - Bob Williamson
Checklists of all known "deaf and dumb" type punch tickets from 1933 onwards.

Part 1 - Tram and Trolleybus	£3.50
Part 2 - Central Buses	£3.50
Part 3 - Country Buses and Green Line Coaches	£2.50
Part 4 - Prepaids	£3.50
Part 5 - Miscellaneous	£3.50

London in 1997 - Brian Pask
Comprehensive survey of tickets and ticket systems in the Capital, covering bus, tube, rail and river services. **£2.50**

INTIS - Brian Boddy
The British Rail Intermediate Ticket Issuing System: a comprehensive guide in two volumes. (*) **£8.00**

Greater Manchester in 1998/9 - Paul J Smith and Brian Hughes
Comlete survey of tickets and ticket systems, covering bus, tram and rail. (*) **£4.50**

The Tickets of the Grimsby & Immingham Electric Railway - Brian Pask
All known tickets described with numerous illustrations, faretables and map. (*) **£4.75**

The Tickets of Hants & Dorset Motor Services 1920-1987 - Part 1 - Punch Tickets - Andrew Waller
Exhaustive history detailing all known punch tickets. Fully-illustrated with tickets, faretables and two maps. (*) **£5.50**

* including illustrations in colour

All prices include postage and packing. Order from the Publication Sales Officer:

Steve Skeavington [X]
6 Breckbank,
Forest Town,
Mansfield,
NG19 0PZ

The Transport Ticket Society

..... offers something for everyone interested in the study and collection of transport tickets, whether casual collector or serious student:

- Monthly, illustrated *Journal* with ticket news from the UK and around the world, articles on tickets, both historical and present-day, and much more.
- Regular distributions of obsolete transport tickets from the UK and overseas.
- Ticket exchange pools, circuits and postal auctions.
- Publications on tickets and related topics.
- Extensive library of ticket and transport items.
- Regular meetings in London, Manchester and Birmingham.

For a *FREE* sample Journal and membership details, send two first-class stamps to the Membership Secretary:

Courtney Haydon [X]
4 Gladridge Close
Earley, Reading
RG6 7DL

E-Mail: courtney@gladridgecl.demon.co.uk

http://www.btinternet.com/~transport.ticket